LINCOLN CHRISTIAN COLLEGE AND SEMINARY
THE FIRST AMERICAN REVOLUTION

Clinton Rossiter is John L. Senior Professor of American Institutions at Cornell University, and has also been Pitt Professor of American History at Cambridge University. His books include The Supreme Court and the Commander in Chief, Constitutional Dictatorship, The American Presidency, Parties and Politics in America, Marxism: The View from America, Conservatism in America, and Seedtime of the Republic, for which he received the Bancroft Prize, the Woodrow Wilson Foundation Award, and the prize of the Institute of Early American History and Culture.

Mr. Rossiter has been a consultant to the Ford and Rockefeller Foundations, is general editor of the series of books on "Communism in American Life" sponsored by the Fund for the Republic, and was a contributor to Goals for Americans, the Report of the President's Commission on National Goals (1960).

CLINTON ROSSITER

THE FIRST AMERICAN REVOLUTION

*The American Colonies on the
Eve of Independence*

A HARVEST BOOK
Harcourt, Brace & World, Inc.
New York

This book is a revised version of Part I of
Seedtime of the Republic.

ISBN 0-15-631121-6

X Y Z

PRINTED IN THE UNITED STATES OF AMERICA

But what do we mean by the American Revolution? Do we mean the American war? The Revolution was effected before the war commenced. The Revolution was in the minds and hearts of the people. . . . This radical change in the principles, opinions, sentiments, and affections of the people, was the real American Revolution.

—JOHN ADAMS, 1818

CONTENTS

For an extensive bibliographical and documentary annotation of these chapters, see pages 457-499 of *Seedtime of the Republic*.

THE FIRST AMERICAN REVOLUTION

I

England in the Wilderness: The Colonists and Their World

———❦———

In the year 1765 there lived along the American sea-board 1,450,000 white and 400,000 Negro subjects of King George III of England. The area of settlement stretched from the Penobscot to the Altamaha and extended inland, by no means solidly, to the Appalachian barrier. Within this area flourished thirteen separate political communities, subject immediately or ultimately to the authority of the Crown, but enjoying in fact large powers of self-government. Life was predominantly rural, the economy agrarian, religion Protestant, descent English, and politics the concern of men of property.

To the best of the average man's knowledge, whether his point of observation was in the colonies or England, all but a handful of these Americans were contented subjects of George III. It was hard for them to be continually enthusiastic about a sovereign or mother country so far away, yet there were few signs that the imperial bonds were about to chafe so roughly. Occasionally statements appeared in print or official correspondence accusing the colonists of republicanism, democracy, and a hankering for independence, but these could be written off as the scoldings of overfastidious travelers or frustrated agents of the royal will. Among the ruling classes sentiments of loyalty to the Crown were strongly held and eloquently expressed, while the attitude of the mass of

men was not much different from that of the plain
people of England: a curious combination of indifference and obeisance. Benjamin Franklin, who had more
firsthand information about the colonies than any
other man, could later write in all sincerity, "I never
had heard in any Conversation from any Person drunk
or sober, the least Expression of a wish for a Separation, or Hint that such a Thing would be advanta-
geous to America."

Yet in the summer and fall of this same year the
colonists shook off their ancient habits of submission
in the twinkling of an eye and stood revealed as almost an alien people. The passage of the Stamp Act
was greeted by an overwhelming refusal to obey, especially among colonial leaders who saw ruin in its
provisions—lawyers, merchants, planters, printers,
and ministers. Although the flame of resistance was
smothered by repeal of the obnoxious act, the next
ten years were at best a smoldering truce. In 1775
the policies of Lord North forced a final appeal to
arms, and enough Americans answered it to bring off
a successful war of independence.

Dozens of able historians have inquired into the
events and forces that drove this colonial people to
armed rebellion. Except among extreme patriots and
equally extreme economic determinists, fundamental
agreement now prevails on the immediate causes of
the American Revolution. Less attention has been devoted to the question: What made this people ripe
for rebellion, or, more exactly, what was there about
the continental colonies in 1765 that made them so
willing to engage in open defiance of a major imperial
policy?

One answer, perhaps the best and certainly the
best-known, was volunteered in 1818 by John Adams,
himself a cause of the American Revolution: "The
Revolution was effected before the war commenced.
The Revolution was in the minds and hearts of the

people. . . . This radical change in the principles, opinions, sentiments, and affections of the people, was the real American Revolution." What Adams seems to have argued was that well before Lexington and Concord there existed a collective outlook called the American mind, a mind whose chief characteristics, so we learn in other parts of his writings, were self-reliance, patriotism, practicality, and love of liberty, with liberty defined as freedom from alien dictation. It was the alien dictation of North, Townshend, Grenville, and the other shortsighted ministers of a shortsighted king that forced the American mind to assert itself boldly for the first time.

Adams did not find it necessary to describe in detail the long-range forces that had produced this mind, perhaps because that extraordinary student of political realities, Edmund Burke, had already given so perceptive a description. In his magnificent speech on conciliation with the colonies March 22, 1775, Burke singled out "six capital sources" to account for the American "love of freedom," that "fierce spirit of liberty" which was "stronger in the English colonies probably than in any other people of the earth": their English descent; their popular forms of government; "religion in the northern provinces"; "manners in the southern"; education, especially in the law; and "the remoteness of the situation from the first mover of government. Implicit in Burke's praise of the American spirit of liberty, as in Adams's recollection of it, was a recognition that this liberty rested on firm and fertile ground, that the colonists enjoyed in fact as well as in spirit a measure of opportunity and self-direction almost unique in the annals of mankind.

The grand thesis of American history toward which Adams and Burke were groping, not altogether blindly, was rounded off by Alexis de Tocqueville a half-century after the Revolution. With one of his most brilliant flashes of insight De Tocqueville revealed the unique nature of the American Republic: "The great advantage of the Americans is that they have arrived at a state of democracy without having to endure a democratic revolution" or, to state the thesis in terms of 1776, the Americans, unlike most revolutionists in history, already enjoyed the liberty for which they were fighting. The "real American Revolution" was over and done with before the Revolution began. The first revolution alone made the second possible.

My purpose in writing this book is to provide an extended commentary in support of Adams, Burke, and de Tocqueville—not that this glorious threesome needs support from anyone. I accept with practically no reservations the notion that the American Revolution was wholly different in character and purpose from the French, Russian, and almost all other revolutions, and I ascribe this difference largely to the plain truth that the Americans had no need and thus no intention to "make the world over." By 1765 their world had already been made over as thoroughly as most sensible men—most sensible white men, to be sure—could imagine or expect. Americans had never known or had long since begun to abandon feudal tenures, a privilege-ridden economy, centralized and despotic government, religious intolerance, and hereditary stratification. Americans had achieved and were prepared to defend with their blood a society more open, an economy more fluid, a religion more tolerant, and a government more popular than anything Europeans would know for decades to come. The goal of the rebellious colonists was largely to consolidate, then expand by cautious stages, the large measure of liberty and prosperity that was already part of their way of life.

This, then, is an account of the American way of life in 1765 and a reckoning of the historical forces that had helped to create a people devoted to liberty and qualified for independence. I wish to make clear that I hold no unusual ideas about the influence of environment on either the institutions or ethics of human freedom. Certainly I would not attempt to weigh each of the many physical and human-directed forces that shaped the destiny of the American colonies, or to establish a precise cause-and-effect relationship between any one force or set of forces and any one value or set of values. What I plan to do is simply to describe the total environment as one overwhelmingly favorable to the rise of liberty and to single out those forces which seemed most influential in creating this environment. Before I proceed to examine these forces and the new world they were shaping, I think it necessary to point to four all-pervading features of the colonial experience that were hastening the day of liberty, independence, and democracy. Over only one of these massive forces did the colonists or English authorities have the slightest degree of control, and the political wisdom that was needed to keep it in tight rein simply did not exist in empires of that time.

I

The first ingredient of American liberty was the heritage from England. Burke acknowledged this "capital source" in words that his countrymen could understand but apparently not act upon.

The people of the colonies are descendants of Englishmen. England, Sir, is a nation which still I hope respects, and formerly adored, her freedom. The colonists emigrated from you when this part of your character was most predominant; and they took this bias and direction the moment they parted from your hands. They are therefore not only devoted to liberty, but to liberty according to English ideas, and on English principles.

"Wee humbly pray," wrote the General Assembly of Rhode Island to the Board of Trade in 1723, "that their Lordships will believe wee have a Tincture of the ancient British Blood in our veines." The colonists had considerably more than a tincture: at least seven in ten were English in blood, and virtually all their institutions, traditions, ideas, and laws were English in origin and inspiration. The first colonists had brought over both the good and evil of seventeenth-century England. The good had been toughened and in several instances improved; much of the bad had been jettisoned under frontier conditions. As a result of this interaction of heredity and environment, the eighteenth-century American was simply a special brand of Englishman. When it pleased him he could be more English than the English, and when it pleased him most was any occurrence in which questions of liberty and self-government were at issue. In a squabble over the question of a fixed salary between Governor Joseph Dudley and the Massachusetts Assembly, the latter could state without any sense of pretension:

It hath been the Priviledge from Henry the third & confirmed by Edward the first, & in all Reigns unto this Day, granted, & is now allowed to be the just & unquestionable Right of the Subject, to raise when & dispose of how they see Cause, any Sums of money by Consent of Parliament, the which Priviledge We her Majesty's Loyal and Dutiful Subjects have lived in the Enjoym^t of, & do hope always to enjoy the same, under Our most gracious Queen Ann & Successors, & shall ever endeavour to discharge the Duty incumbent on us; But humbly conceive the Stating of perpetual Salaries not agreable to her Majesty's Interests in this Province, but prejudicial to her Majesty's good Subjects.

Southerners were, if anything, more insistent. In 1735 the South Carolina legislature resolved:

That His Majesty's subjects in this province are entitled to all the liberties and privileges of Englishmen . . . [and]

that the Commons House of Assembly in South Carolina, by the laws of England and South Carolina, and ancient usage and custom, have all the rights and privileges pertaining to Money bills that are enjoyed by the British House of Commons.

And the men of the frontier, who were having the same trouble with assemblies that assemblies were having with governors, made the echo ring.

1st. We apprehend, as Free-Men and English Subjects, we have an indisputable Title to the same Privileges and Immunities with his Majesty's other Subjects, who reside in the interior Counties of Philadelphia, Chester and Bucks, and therefore ought not to be excluded from an equal Share with them in the very important Privilege of Legislation.

These were the words of men who made much of the English tie, even when, as in the last of these instances, most of them were Scotch-Irish or German. Their traditions—representative government, supremacy of law, constitutionalism, liberty of the subject— belonged to them as Englishmen. Their institutions, especially the provincial assembly, were often looked upon as sound to the extent that they conformed to English models, or at least to colonial interpretations or recollections of those models. The rights for which they contended were not the natural rights of all men but the ancient rights of Englishmen. "It is no Little Blessing of God," said Cotton Mather to the Massachusetts Assembly in 1700, "that we are a part of the *English Nation.*"

Throughout the colonial period the English descent and attitudes of the great majority of Americans gave impetus to their struggles for liberty. It is a momentous fact of American history that until 1776 it was a chapter in English history as well. Just as England in 1765 was ahead of the Continent in the struggle for law and liberty, so America, this extraordinary part of England, was even further ahead, not

least because most of its leading inhabitants thought
of themselves as Englishmen. Such men would not
easily be cheated or argued out of their heritage—a
truth that Burke did his best to advertise:

The temper and character which prevail in our colonies
are, I am afraid, unalterable by any human art. We cannot,
I fear, falsify the pedigree of this fierce people, and persuade
them that they are not sprung from a nation in whose veins
the blood of freedom circulates. The language in which
they would hear you tell them this tale would detect the
imposition; your speech would betray you. An Englishman
is the unfittest person on earth to argue another Englishman
into slavery.

The clash of imperial policy and colonial self-reliance is almost always productive of the spirit of liberty. This is especially true if the policy of the parent
state is conceived purely in its own interests, and if the
colonists are men of high political aptitude and proud
descent. Such was the pattern of Anglo-American relations in the colonial period. From the time of the
earliest settlement, which like all the important settlements was the result of private initiative, English
and American opinions on the political and economic
status of the colonies were in sharp conflict.

The conduct of colonial affairs by the English government rested on these assumptions: The colonies
were dependents of the parent state. Since their
interests were subordinate to those of England, the
welfare of the latter was to be the one concern of
all agencies charged with governing them. They were
therefore to serve, apparently forever, as a source of
wealth and support for the land out of which their
inhabitants had departed. If the English government
had acted on these assumptions consistently throughout the colonial period, the contrasting ideas of the
colonists would have had less chance to strike deep
root. But confusion at the beginning, domestic troubles in the middle, and "salutary neglect" throughout

most of this period permitted the colonists to build not only a theory but a condition of self-government. And it was this condition, of course, as some perceptive Englishmen were aware, that helped the colonies develop into prizes worth retaining by force of arms. The interests of England were, in this important sense, fatally self-contradictory.

The views of the colonists on their place in the imperial structure were somewhat mixed, ranging from the arrogant independence asserted by Massachusetts in the seventeenth century to the abject dependence argued by a handful of Tory apologists in the eighteenth. In general, the colonial attitude was one looking to near-equality in the present and some sort of full partnership in the future, all within the confines of a benevolent and protecting empire. The colonist acknowledged that for certain diplomatic and commercial purposes his destiny would rest for some time to come in the hands of men in London. But in all other matters, especially in that of political self-determination, he considered himself a "freeborn subject of the Crown of England." Theories of the origin and nature of the colonial assemblies are a good example of these divergent views. In English eyes the assemblies were founded by royal grant and existed at royal pleasure; in American eyes they existed as a matter of right. The Board of Trade looked upon them as inferior bodies enjoying rule-making powers under the terms of their charters; the men of Virginia and Massachusetts looked upon them as miniature Houses of Commons with power to make all laws they could get away with in practice. The struggle between these assemblies and the royal governors sent to control them was the focus of conflict of colonial and imperial interests.

Had Parliament not decided to intrude its authority into colonial affairs, the old-fashioned imperial views of the English authorities and the prophetic

self-governing claims of the American colonists might
have coexisted for decades without producing a violent break. The tardy policies of stern control initi-
ated by the Grenville ministry brought this long-
standing conflict fully into the open. In the years
before 1765 the push-and-pull of imperialism and
home rule had been a spur to the growth of liberty
in the colonies. In the next decade it ignited a rebellion.

II

Let us hear again from the member for Bristol.

The last cause of this disobedient spirit in the colonies is
hardly less powerful than the rest, as it is not merely moral,
but laid deep in the natural constitution of things. Three
thousand miles of ocean lie between you and them. No con-
trivance can prevent the effect of this distance in weakening
government. Seas roll, and months pass, between the order
and the execution; and the want of a speedy explanation of
a single point is enough to defeat a whole system. . . . In
large bodies, the circulation of power must be less vigorous
at the extremities. Nature has said it. . . . This is the immutable condition, the eternal law, of extensive and detached empire.

This harsh fact of geography, the remoteness of
the colonies, squared the difference between imperial
purpose and colonial aspiration. The early colonists,
thrown willy-nilly on their own devices, developed
habits of self-government and passed them on to their
descendants. The descendants, still just as far if not
farther from London, fell naturally into an attitude of
provincialism well suited to their condition but cor-
rosive of empire. The lack of contact between one
colony and another, the result of distance and unbelievably bad roads, allowed each to develop on its own.
The diversity in character of the key colonies of
Virginia, Massachusetts, New York, and Pennsylvania

made a mockery of any notion of uniform imperial policy.

Worst of all from the imperial point of view, the ill effects of the inconsistency, inefficiency, corruption, stupidity, arrogance, and ignorance displayed to some degree at all times and to a perilous degree at some times by the English authorities were doubled and redoubled by the rolling seas and passing months. English laxity in enforcing the Navigation Acts and colonial habits of disobeying them were one instance of the extent to which three thousand miles of ocean could water down a policy of strict control. The technique of royal disallowance, which seemed so perfectly designed to keep the colonial assemblies in check, was likewise weakened by the mere fact of distance. For example, the disallowance in 1706 of two New Hampshire judiciary acts passed in 1699 and 1701 was never reported properly to the province, and the judiciary in that colony continued to function under these laws for a half century. And the royal governor, the linchpin of empire, was a far more accommodating fellow in Boston or Charleston than he appeared in his commissions and instructions issued from London. A governor like Sir Matthew Johnson of North Carolina, whose reports to the Board of Trade went astray four years in a row, could not have been much of a buffer against colonial urges to independence. When we realize that no regular mail-service of any kind existed until 1755, and that war disrupted communications more than one-third of the time between 1689 and 1763, we can understand how the ocean was at once a highway to freedom and a barrier to imperialism. Rarely in history have the laws of geopolitics worked so powerfully for liberty.

Had Burke ever lived in the colonies, he might have listed still another "capital source" to explain the rise of liberty in America, and thus have anticipated Frederick Jackson Turner and his celebrated thesis. We need not go all the way with Turner—"American democracy is fundamentally the outcome of the experiences of the American people in dealing with the West"—to acknowledge the significance of the frontier in early American history. Whatever the extent of that influence in the nineteenth century, in the seventeenth and eighteenth centuries—when America was one vast frontier and perhaps one in three Americans a frontiersman at some time in his life—it was clearly of the first importance. If we may take the word "frontier" to mean not only the line of farthest settlement to the west, but also the primitive conditions of life and thought which extended throughout the colonies in the seventeenth century and continued to prevail in many areas east of the Appalachians during most of the eighteenth, we may point to at least a half-dozen indications of the influence of the American environment.

First, the frontier impeded the transfer to America of outworn attitudes and institutions. The wilderness frustrated completely such attempts to plant feudalism in America as the schemes of Sir Ferdinando Gorges and the stillborn Fundamental Constitutions of Carolina, and everywhere archaic laws and customs were simplified, liberalized, or rudely abandoned. In the matter of church-state relations the frontier was especially influential as a decentralizing and democratizing force. The positive result of this process of sloughing off the old ways was an increase in mobility, experimentation, and self-reliance among the settlers.

The wilderness demanded of those who would conquer it that they spend their lives in unremitting toil. Unable to devote any sizable part of their energies to government, the settlers insisted that government let them alone and perform its severely limited tasks at the amateur level. The early American definition of liberty as freedom *from* government was given added popularity and meaning by frontier conditions. It was a new and invigorating experience for tens of thousands of Englishmen, Germans, and Scotch-Irish to be able to build a home where they would at last be "let alone."

The frontier produced, in ways that Turner and his followers have made clear, a new kind of individual and new doctrines of individualism. The wilderness did not of itself create democracy; indeed, it often encouraged the growth of ideas and institutions hostile to it. But it did help produce some of the raw materials of American democracy—self-reliance, social fluidity, simplicity, equality, dislike of privilege, optimism, and devotion to liberty. At the same time, it emphasized the importance of voluntary co-operation. The group, too, had its uses on the frontier, whether for defense or barn-raising or cornhusking. The phrases "free association," "mutual subjection," and "the consent of the governed" were given new content in the wilderness.

Next, the fact that wages were generally higher and working conditions better in the colonies than in England did much to advance the cause of liberty. The reason for this happy condition was a distinct shortage of labor, and a prime reason for the shortage was land for the asking. The frontier population was made up of thousands of men who had left the seaboard to toil for themselves in the great forest. The results of this constant migration were as important for the seaboard as they were for the wilderness.

From the beginning the frontier was an area of protest and thus a nursery of republican notions. Under-represented in assemblies that made a habit of overtaxing them, scornful of the privileges and leadership assumed by the tidewater aristocracy, resentful of attempts to saddle them with unwanted ministers and officials, the men of the back country were in fact if not in print the most determined radicals of the colonial period. If their quaint and strangely deferential protests contributed very little to the literature of a rising democracy, they nevertheless made more popular the arguments for liberty and self-government.

Finally, all these factors combined to give new force to the English heritage of law, liberty, and self-government. The over-refined and often archaic institutions that the settlers brought along as part of their intellectual baggage were thrust once again into the crucible of primitive conditions. If these institutions emerged in shapes that horrified royal governors, they were nevertheless more simple, workable, and popular than they had been for several centuries in England. The laws and institutions of early Rhode Island or North Carolina would not have worked in more civilized societies, but they had abandoned most of their outworn features and were ready to develop along American lines. The hardworking, long-suffering men and women of the frontier—"People a litle wilful Inclined to doe when and how they please or not at al"—were themselves a primary force in the rise of colonial self-government.

The English descent and heritage of the colonists, the conflict of imperial and colonial interests, the rolling ocean, the all-pervading frontier—these were the "forces-behind-the-forces" that shaped the history of the colonies and spurred the peaceful revolution that preceded the bloody one of 1776. Of these forces we shall speak or think on almost every page of this book.

III

The colonists were not completely at the mercy of their environment. Much of the environment was of their own making; and if circumstances were favorable to the rise of liberty, they did not relieve the colonists of the formidable task of winning it for themselves. The condition of liberty in 1765 was in large part the work of men determined to be free, and the questions thus arise: Who were these men who talked so much of their rights and privileges? Whence came they to America, and how did they fare?

The attempt of historians and genealogists to decipher the national origins of the colonists has led to confusion and controversy, first, because of a manifest lack of statistics, and second, because of the temptation, apparently too strong even for some of our best-intentioned scholars, to magnify the numbers and accomplishments of one nationality at the expense of all others. Nevertheless, the development of more reliable historical techniques and a more equitable historical spirit has created a broad area of consensus on the composition and distribution of the population.

It is now generally agreed that almost all immigrants to the colonies came from the middle and lower classes. "The rich stay in Europe," wrote Crèvecoeur; "it is only the middling and the poor that emigrate." The myths of aristocratic lineage die hard, especially in Cavalier country, but diaries, shipping lists, and court minutes tell us in no uncertain terms of the simple origins of even the most haughty families of New York and Virginia. This does not mean that early America was a land of rogues and poor servant-girls England and the Continent sent over thousands upon thousands of substantial, intelligent, propertied men and women. Yet fully half the people who came to the colonies could not pay their own passage, and gentleman immigrants, even in the seventeenth century, were amazingly few.

As a matter of fact, those twentieth-century Americans who like to go searching for an ancestor among the gentry of East Anglia may wind up with three or four among the riffraff of Old Bailey. Probably thirty to forty thousand convicts were shipped from England to the colonies in the eighteenth century, a fact that inspired Dr. Johnson's famous growl: "Sir, they are a race of convicts, and ought to be content with anything we allow them short of hanging." Their behavior in the colonies, especially in unhappy Virginia and Maryland, moved Franklin to offer America's rattlesnakes to England as the only appropriate return. Not only did transported convicts commit a large proportion of the crimes in eighteenth-century America, but their presence did much to degrade the servant class and make a callous society even more callous. The mother country's insistence on dumping "the dregs, the excrescence of England" in the colonies was a major item in the catalogue of American grievances, especially since the Privy Council vetoed repeatedly the acts through which the colonies sought to protect themselves.

Well before 1765 the colonies had begun to take on a pattern of national origins that was "characteristically American": They looked to one country for their language, institutions, and paramount culture, but to many for their population. Americans were predominantly English in origin, but they were also Scotch, Irish, German, French, Swiss, Dutch, Swedish, and African. It is impossible to fix precisely the proportions of each nationality in the total white population of 1765; the necessary statistics are simply not available. These general percentages are about as accurate as can be expected: English, 65 to 70 per cent; Scots and Scotch-Irish, 12 to 15 per cent; Germans, 6 to 9 per cent; Irish, 3 to 5 per cent; Dutch 3 per cent; all others 3 to 5 per cent. Out of a total population of 1,850,000, probably 400,000 were Negroes and mulattoes.

The eighteenth rather than seventeenth century was the era of immigration and expansion. The early migrations to Massachusetts and Virginia, astonishing as they must have seemed at the time, were trickles when contrasted with the flood of men that poured into the colonies in the peaceful stretches of the eighteenth century. The natural increase of population was also stepped up in the eighteenth century, a phenomenon to which Franklin called attention with a homely but trustworthy example: "Dr. Elliot writes me, that in their Town of Killingworth in which few or no Strangers come to settle, the People double every 15 Years, as appears by examining the Train band Lists taken annually."

These approximate figures of the total population of the colonies are helpful to bear in mind:

1650	50,000
1675	140,000
1700	240,000
1730	650,000
1750	1,150,000
1765	1,850,000

I turn now to a brief reckoning of the national elements in this population and begin, of course, with the English majority. The fact that America's career as asylum of the oppressed of many nations was well under way in 1765 should not obscure the predominantly English character of the colonial population. Seven in ten were of English blood, almost nine in ten were British. Although immigration from England tapered off sharply after 1689, the high rate of natural increase among the early families of New England and the tidewater had by 1750 produced a basic stock of perhaps one million English-Americans. It was these people, of course, who controlled America—politically, linguistically, culturally, and institutionally. The Dutch, French, Germans, and Scotch-Irish were energizing transfusions, but the English were, from beginning to end, the body and blood of colonial society. Even Pennsylvania, the most thoroughly cosmopolitan colony, had almost as many people of English descent as of all other nationalities put together. This is a plain truth that historians of this or that national group would do well to keep in mind.

From the North of Britain came two elements in the population: the Scots, who drifted in directly from their home country throughout the latter part of the colonial period, and the so-called Scotch-Irish, or the "Scots settled in Ireland," who had been living in the North of Ireland since early in the seventeenth century. The Scots, an unpopular people in colonial days, came from both lowlands and highlands. The Scotch clergyman, factor, and schoolmaster from the lowlands—all familiar figures in the colonies —were often quite English in character and outlook even before emigration. Highlanders, who left Scotland in largest numbers in the hard times after the rebellions of 1715 and 1746, were a more alien element, generally preferring to settle in their own isolated communities. Wherever he came from and wherever he settled, the industrious Scot was a man who fitted naturally into the American scene.

The Scotch-Irish of Ulster, who numbered thousands of Englishmen and Irishmen along with the predominant Scots, began to come to America around 1715. These people, for the most part lowlanders, had first been settled in northern Ireland in the reign of James I, had added to their numbers after 1685, and had prospered entirely too much for their own good. Harassed repeatedly by acts of Parliament that excluded their products, the Scotch-Irish were driven to seek a refuge in America. They came by tens of thousands, first to New England, where they were not very enthusiastically welcomed, then to Pennsylvania and the frontier counties to the south. The old colonists called them Irish, but they called themselves British. Said the inhabitants of Londonderry, New Hampshire, in 1720: "We were surprised to hear ourselves termed *Irish* people, when we so frequently ventured our all for the British Crown and Liberties against the Irish Papists." (It was a "Scot settled in Ireland" who first insisted that birth in a stable does not make a man a horse.) Many Scotch-Irish came as indentured servants, but as servants who had every intention of ending up free, self-supporting farmers. By 1765 there were several hundred settlements in the western counties in which Scotch-Irish held sway. Natural-born frontiersmen, these hardy people were the most powerful national influence for western expansion, religious dissent, and democratic politics in the eighteenth century.

Catholic or southern Irish, as distinguished from Calvinist or northern Scotch-Irish, were also to be found in every colony, but especially in Maryland and Pennsylvania. Most of them came as individuals or in families, often abandoning their religion in order to win a friendlier reception. The average southern Irish immigrant failed to preserve his national identity. The fact that the Scotch, Irish, and English strands of the total Irish migration of the eighteenth century are hopelessly snarled has persuaded some pariots to make ridiculous claims for the "pure" Irish. Yet the claims of the Scotch-Irish must not be pushed too far in the other direction. At least 20 per cent of the "Irish" of the eighteenth-century migration must have actually been Irish in national origin.

The largest national element with a character distinctly alien to the dominant English strain was the German population in the middle and Southern colonies. Poverty, war, and religious persecution drove so many thousands of Rhinelanders to Pennsylvania in the eighteenth century that Franklin and others predicted a Germanic future for the colony. In upstate New York, the western counties of the South, and above all in Pennsylvania, Germans settled in great swarms, more often than not retaining their language, customs, and culture. Although they took a small part in the political and social life of the colonies, their superior farming skill, thrift, and industry made them important in the economy, while their multiform Protestantism was a spur to religious liberty. Pennsylvania was the breadbasket of the American Revolution not least because it was one-third German. Many a colonial official echoed the sentiments of Governor Phipps, who recommended to the Massachusetts Assembly in 1750 that it encourage the immigration of a people so well fitted to "teach us by their Example those most necessary and excellent Arts for encreasing our Wealth, I mean Frugality and Diligence; in which at present we are exceedingly defective."

Perhaps fifteen to twenty thousand Swiss migrated to America from the German-speaking cantons between 1700 and 1765, fully half of them arriving in the decade 1734-1744. Pennsylvania and the Carolinas were the main destinations of these valuable immigrants, most of whom were regarded as another of the numerous breeds of German immigrant. A few French-speaking Swiss were also in the colonies.

It has been variously estimated that between twenty and forty thousand French Protestants settled in the colonies after the revocation of the Edict of Nantes in 1685, most of them coming by way of England and Holland. Several features made this migration one of the most influential in colonial times: the way in which the French scattered themselves throughout the colonies; the high proportion of gentle blood, intelligence, and professional skill they brought with them; and the almost effortless manner in which they were assimilated into the colonial population. In religion, speech, and culture the

French Huguenot became an authentic English-American. Charleston and New Rochelle are perhaps the most interesting places in which to study the assimilation of this people whose character was so well attuned to American methods and aspirations. It is fascinating to read the records of New Rochelle and see how easily the Huguenots took to the town-meeting form of government. *Visiteurs de fænces, assesseurs, connestables,* and "Town Mens" all did their jobs as if they had been Yankees born. The great names of Bowdoin, Revere, Bernon, Faneuil, Jay, De Lancey, Manigault, and Laurens are proof of the disproportionate influence of these few thousand exiles in the shaping of a new nationality. In addition to the Huguenots, perhaps five thousand Acadian French were deported and scattered along the coast in 1755, but their influence in the original colonies was negligible.

The story of New Netherland and New Amsterdam is such common American property that it is easy to overestimate the influence of Dutch blood and culture in the development of the colonies. It is generally agreed that there were only ten thousand Dutch in the colonies in 1700, that perhaps fifty to sixty thousand persons had predominantly Dutch blood in 1765, and that in eighteenth-century New York and New Jersey, where this stock was concentrated, roughly 15 to 20 per cent of the total white population could be classified as Dutch. Dutch immigration and influence were largely confined to the seventeenth century and the middle colonies. Dutch institutions were quickly scrapped after the English conquest of 1664, while the language, although some Hudson River farmers and Dutch Reformed pastors clung to it tenaciously, was in decline long before the end of the colonial period. The main contributions of the Dutch to the colonies were a good national stock, some expressive words, and a policy of colonization that made New York a cosmopolitan city from the beginning. The first permanent settlers of New Netherland were thirty families of Protestant, French-speaking Walloons from the southern Netherlands. Comparatively few Dutch were prepared to leave home and settle permanently in the new world, yet those who did fathered a breed of typical colonists. An English nobleman observed in 1765, "The people of Albany are mostly descended of low Dutch, and carry down with them, the true and characteristick marks of their Native Country, Vizt an unwearied attention to their own personal and particular Interests, and an abhorrence to all superior powers."

Some ten to fifteen thousand colonists in 1765 had predominantly Swedish blood. Most of these were descendants of the few hundred settlers of New Sweden on the Delaware, which was founded as a fur-trading center in 1638 and was taken over by the Dutch in 1655. Although many of these sturdy farmers and traders migrated to other parts of the middle colonies, the original area of settlement maintained cultural and ecclesiastical ties with the homeland well into the eighteenth century. Over the years the Swedes proved to be a reasonably assimilable national element, as did also the small number of Finns and even smaller sprinkling of Danes who helped plant the tiny colony at Fort Christina.

The total number of Jews in the colonies in 1765 could not have been more than 1,500, most of them Spanish or Portuguese in immediate origin. Newport, New York, Charleston, and Savannah were the principal havens of this trading people, but they could also be found in individual families or tiny groups through all the colonies. Jews suffered the expected social and political discrimination, but in the field of business they were first-class citizens. Many of them lived, as one traveler observed of the New York Jews, in highly respectable style.

They have a synagogue and houses; and great country seats of their own property, and are allowed to keep shops in town. They have likewise several ships, which they freight, and send out with their own goods. In fine, they enjoy all the privileges common to the other inhabitants of this town and province.

What Peter Kalm saw he reported correctly, but he did not see enough. The Jew was happy, but his was the limited happiness of a man held at arm's length.

I will have occasion later to discuss the Negro in colonial America, and need therefore mention only a few facts and figures. There were perhaps 400,000 Negroes in 1765, or slightly more than 20 per cent of the total population. All but forty thousand of this number were concentrated in the colonies south of Pennsylvania, and all but a handful were slaves. The Negro had in no way been assimilated into the population and had been integrated into the white man's society only on the white man's terms. Most important, he had been left by law and custom—and with little popular protest—in a state of ignorance, primitivism, and paganism, a state in which most colonists thought he naturally belonged. The total effect of slavery on the colonies was enormous, yet the white man's bloodlines and culture were hardly disturbed by the Negro's presence.

Only a few thousand Indians lived permanently within the settled areas in 1765. Despite the pretty story of Pocahontas and John Rolfe, there was very little mixing of Indian and European blood. The white man's agriculture, commerce, road system, and language owed varying debts to the Indian tribes, but the chief influence of these native Americans was as a bar to easy westward expansion. Far too much blood was shed at the points of contact between two contradictory ways of life to make the myth of the "noble savage" a part of colonial culture.

What was the total effect on society, culture, and government of this influx of nationalities into the American settlement? I will attempt to evaluate English influence at several points in the course of this book. But what of the other nationalities, especially the Scotch-Irish and Germans? What did they do to reshape or improve the dominant English strain?

First, the melting pot had only just begun to heat up in the latter part of the eighteenth century. Crèvecoeur's example of the English-French-Dutch family "whose present four sons have now four wives of four different nations" was a phenomenon more prophetic of the Republic than typical of the colonies. The great process of national fusion had made little progress by 1765. Assimilation into the English stock rather than the creation of a new people was the result of such intermarriage as took place in colonial times. Nor were all the ingredients yet in the pot; the essential racial (Teutonic-Celtic) and religious (Protestant) unity of the population must not be overlooked.

The arrival of non-English immigrants did much to weaken the hold of the mother country. The newcomer wanted to be as loyal as anyone else, but his allegiance to the Crown could have little real emotional content. The Germans were inclined to be conservatively neutral about English dominion; the Scots and Irish were, for all the loyal humility that oozed from their petitions, innately hostile to the Georges and their agents. They lacked, as one traveler put it, the "same filial attachment" to England "which her own immediate offspring have."

Next, the influx of aliens did much to strengthen

the Protestant, dissenting, individualistic character of colonial religion. The Presbyterian, Lutheran, Baptist, and German Pietist churches were the chief beneficiaries of this immigration. The numbers and enthusiasm of these dissenting groups gave a tremendous lift to the cause of religious liberty in the colonies south of Pennsylvania.

The eighteenth-century immigrants helped democratize the political institutions that had been brought over from England and put to work in the wilderness. This was especially true of the Scotch-Irish, whose only quarrel with the representative governments of their adopted colonies was that they were not representative enough. The Germans were inclined to be politically passive; their major contribution to the coming democracy was the support they brought to the middle-class creed of industry, frugality, and self-reliance. The Scotch-Irish, on the other hand, were more politically conscious. If the controlling groups of the coastal counties refused to honor their legitimate claims to participation in public life, this rebuff served only to make their radicalism more insistent. They had little intention of altering the English-American scheme of government, but they did mean to show the world how democratic it could be. The sentiments of "leveling republicanism" were especially active on the Scotch-Irish frontier; here the "real American Revolution" went on apace.

Finally, the mere volume of immigration from Germany and Ireland had a pronounced effect on colonial life. The swarming of these industrious peoples made possible the remarkable expansion in territory and population that marked the eighteenth century in America. If the Scotch-Irishman was America's typical frontiersman, the German was its typical farmer; and between them they made it possible for cities like Philadelphia and towns like Lancaster to grow and flourish. Though they were men of different natures, both sought the same blessing. "And what but LIBERTY, charming LIBERTY, is the resistless Magnet that attracts so many different Nations into that flourishing Colony?"

II

Soil, Sea, and Forest:
The Economy of the Colonies

❦

Through all history man's first concern has been to "make a living," to acquire and use food, shelter, clothing, and physical comforts. Several notable cultures have existed in which the worship of God, the study of war, or the playing of politics seemed to consume most of the time of most people, but even in these the dominance of religion, war, or politics was made possible only by a happy conjunction of economic forces. The paramount influence of economic motives and conditions is apparent at every stage of colonial history. The decline of feudalism and rise of commercial capitalism inspired the great explorations that opened up the Western hemisphere. A host of economic motives—the search for gold and silver, the demand for raw materials, the quest for new markets, the desire for private profit—promoted the settlement of North America and the West Indies. A longing for economic betterment was the compelling force that brought most colonists over the seas, whether from East Anglia in 1630, the Rhineland in 1700, or Ulster in 1720. And the powder train of events that set off the American Revolution was fired and fanned by a series of decisions on commercial policy.

The influence of economic forces on the rise of American liberty was mixed in character and results. Many arrangements and theories—for example, the web of laws, customs, and pressures that controlled the acquisition and tenure of land—seemed often to be working just as powerfully against liberty, self-government, and political equality as for them. In general, however, the story of the colonial economy is one of expansion—in freedom of choice, equality of opportunity, level of productivity, and vitality of competition. It is the story of the origins of the fabled economic system that has shaped the destiny of modern America.

I

The most important fact about the early American economy was that it was a colonial economy, that these thirteen political entities were commercial accessories of a busy empire. The colonial period of American history coincided with the highest development of the English mercantile system; from beginning to end the colonies existed primarily for economic support of the mother country.

Mercantilism, it will be remembered, was a many-sided condition rather than a coherent theory, a kind of economic nationalism nourished on the assumption that the states of Europe were engaged in perpetual commercial war with one another. Although there were as many varieties of mercantile theory as there were mercantilists, the economists of seventeenth- and eighteenth-century England were united in their insistence that the state must control enterprise in the interest of national power and aggrandizement. Internally, this called for elaborate regulation of production and labor. Externally, it called for a fantastic apparatus of law and policy—protective tariffs, embargoes, bounties, prohibitions, navigation acts, treaties, and monopolies—all designed to achieve a favorable balance of trade, "to sell more to strangers yearly than wee consume of theirs in value." Most important for American history, mercantile doctrine called for settlement and exploitation of overseas colonies.

In the old colonial system a colony was to be a colony in the most obvious sense of the word: a perpetually subordinate agricultural and extractive area that served the mother country as a source of raw materials, a safety valve for excess or unwanted population, and a market for finished goods. The perfect colony under the mercantile system was one in which "the inhabitants . . . wear not a rag of their own manufacturing; drive not a nail of their own forging; eat not out of a platter or cup of their own making; nay . . . produce not even bread to eat." The perfect colony, of course, never existed, nor were English colonial policy and English mercantilism always synonymous. Yet the general assumptions of mercantilism governed the mother country's policy throughout the crucial period of American development. England always feared and often frustrated the rise of an American economy that would compete with rather than supplement her own economy.

The colonists, too, were mercantilists. The men of Massachusetts and Virginia, like the men of London and Bristol, were beneficiaries of a social heritage that looked upon government control of economic activity as an ethical and practical necessity. The attempt of certain defenders of "rugged individualism" to project laissez-faire capitalism back to Plymouth and Jamestown is historical nonsense. The early colonists, whose economic theories were a compound of declining medievalism and rising mercantilism, acknowledged government intervention as the one sure cure for the plague of economic problems besetting their infant communities. Their descendants shook off the medieval but not the mercantile doctrines of political economy, and not until the middle of the eighteenth century did laissez-faire policies begin to challenge this long-standing tradition of public regulation of business. The Revolution touched off a major revival of economic controls, thereby demonstrating that the colonists were not opposed to mercantilism except of the imperial variety.

Evidences of domestic mercantilism fill the records of town and province. Among the problems regulated at one time or another by law and ordinance were the price and quality of commodities like bread, meat, bricks, firewood, and leather; fares charged by public conveyances, storage and wharfage rates, and fees for such public services as corn-grinding and slaughtering; licenses, fees, and wages of millers, carmen, porters, draymen, and smiths; prices of food, drink, and lodging in taverns; and market practices in general, the latter a survival of medieval prohibitions on forestalling, engrossing, and monopolizing the necessities of life. The assemblies passed a multitude of laws governing commerce and manufacturing: tonnage duties, import and export taxes, inspection laws, port regulations, and embargoes, not to mention bounties, monopoly privileges, and subsidies. Nor was this intervention, as is often assumed, confined to the Puritan colonies. Although Massachusetts experimented most purposefully in wage- and price-controls, Virginia and Maryland regulated their major undertaking, the tobacco industry, with force and ingenuity. The attempt to raise agricultural prices by restrictions on production is a legacy from colonial America, not a New Deal invention. Virginia was apparently full of Henry Wallaces.

The intentions of the colonial mercantilists far outran the effectiveness of their laws and ordinances. The people of the colonies, like people all through history, were wonderfully adept at evading economic controls. Nature was too grand, conditions too primitive, government too meager, society too increasingly fluid and secular to permit these controls to be enforced with vigor or continuity. Yet it is a fact to remember, even if it hurts, that throughout the colonial period government regulation and stimulation of the economy were regarded as part of the natural order of things.

The colonial economy was predominantly agrarian, which is exactly what English merchants wanted it to be. Something like eight in ten colonists took their living from the soil. One in ten was engaged in one of the closely allied extractive industries—fishing, lumbering, fur-trading, and the production of naval stores. So completely did soil and forest dominate the lives and occupations of men that in 1765 only five places on the American continent had populations in excess of eight thousand. These cities—Boston, New York, Philadelphia, Newport, Charleston—had probably eighty thousand inhabitants, less than 5 per cent of the total. Commerce, of which there was a great deal, and manufacturing, of which there was very little, were both extensions of the great pursuit of agriculture. Many merchants, fishermen, and craftsmen were themselves part-time cultivators of the soil. The dominance of agriculture had many effects: The land itself was the most important single economic factor in early American history; the colonies would have to pass through a long period of dependence on the mother country before they were able to strike out for themselves; a people quite unprepared for the "curses and vexations" of eighteenth-century urban life were largely spared its ill effects; the land was celebrated as the sure foundation of wealth, virtue, and freedom; politics took on a decidedly rural flavor; the native aristocracy, except in parts of commercial New England, was a landed aristocracy; and the colonial economy was a simple affair in which emphasis rested on self-sufficiency, hard work, and personal independence.

This last point, the simplicity of the colonial economy, demands separate attention. The techniques employed in field, forest, shop, or countinghouse were often so simple as to verge on the primitive. Technology and research had done little in 1650 and not much more in 1750 to distinguish farmer, fisherman, laborer, craftsman, or merchant from his counterpart in feudal times. Only the broadest outlines of specialization and of division of labor were marked out in colonial America. Men were by necessity jacks-of-all-trades, and most of them spent their lives in ceaseless toil. One important result of this absorption in the struggle for existence was the fact that ordinary men were left with little time or energy for politics or political thinking, which therefore remained largely in the keeping of gentry and preachers. These men toiled pretty hard themselves, and few were those who made politics their chief business. This in itself was a blessing for which more than one colonial penman returned thanks to God.

The context of law, custom, and theory in which men carried on this economy of long hours and few rewards was correspondingly simple. However perplexing the rules and problems of commerce may have seemed to a Virginia planter or Boston lawyer-merchant, they exhibited none of the complexity of modern or even of nineteenth-century enterprise. The patterns and social results of taxation are example enough of this state of affairs. Although the deceptively low taxes of 1656 or 1756 were just as hard for a man to pay as those of 1956, the system that taxed him was certainly easier to understand and control.

A corollary of agrarian simplicity was the absence of manufacturing on any but the most restricted and primitive scale. This should occasion no surprise, for the industrial revolution had not come to England itself. Yet the level of manufacturing enterprise divorced from the household was, until the end of the colonial period, far lower in the colonies than in the mother country. Ironworking, flour-milling, wood-preparing, shipbuilding, glassmaking, and other such undertakings were carried on in small and localized units. Nothing resembling a modern factory, not even Peter Hasenclever's ill-fated ironworks in New York and New Jersey, existed in colonial times. Since there was no industry, there were no industrial problems.

The reasons usually advanced to explain the retarded condition of manufacturing go far to describe the colonial economy. Among these were: English laws encouraging agrarian and extractive pursuits and discouraging manufacturing; the difficulties of transportation and communication within the colonies and with the rest of the world, which frustrated the rise of stable markets; a chronic shortage of coin and specie, and the instability and inadequacy of the many forms of paper issues and barter that were employed as substitutes; a lack of surplus capital, and the preference of colonial investors for such traditional ventures as shipping, slaves, and land; the sovereignty of the natural environment, of sea, forest, and soil; the tradition of agriculture as a business and way of life; the high cost and scarcity of labor, the result of an environment in which few men could command wages attractive enough to divert them from the lure of cheap land; the assumption of agrarian thinkers that manufacturing and poverty went always hand in hand; and the absence of socio-economic compulsions that might have led a little sooner to improved methods of craftsmanship, labor-saving machinery, and the beginnings of technology.

Household manufactures, individual crafts, and

small and widely dispersed ventures in converting
iron ore, wood, and wheat to commercial use—this
was the extent of "industry" in colonial America. In
the final reckoning, not English policy but colonial
conditions retarded American industrial development. Toward the end of the colonial period the pace
of industrial progress began to quicken, but the units
established were tiny by modern standards.

II

From inception to independence the colonies were
junior partners in a commercial civilization. Agriculture was the primary pursuit, but except in the pioneering stages it was commercial rather than subsistence farming that occupied most colonists, whether
on large farms or small. The purpose of the colonial
farmer was no different from that of his present-day
descendant: to produce surpluses for sale in the domestic or foreign market. The purpose of his countrymen in town and port was to pay him cash or
barter for these surpluses, convert them or package
them, and ship them off at a profit. The lifeblood of
the colonial economy was trade in agricultural surpluses and other commodities within the colonies and
over the seas. Foreign commerce was a more vital element in the life of this underdeveloped area than it
would have been in an older, more self-sufficient community. Indeed, the welfare of the colonies depended
on foreign trade to a degree hardly understandable to
later generations. The merchants of Boston, Newport, New York, Philadelphia, and Charleston, standing as they did at the meeting point of the coun-
tercurrents of American agricultural products and
English finished goods, were thus the most important
persons in the colonial economy. Their profits and
their leadership in politics and society are not difficult to explain.

The tradition of government regulation of the economy was part of the colonial way of life; laissez-faire arguments were rarely heard in economic debate; manufacturing on any but the most primitive scale was unknown to the American continent. Yet it would be a mistake to overlook the elements of capitalism that had developed in the colonies by 1765, for example, virtually universal private ownership of the means of production, the primacy of the profit motive (in Peter Faneuil's Boston, if not in John Winthrop's), and the use of credit and the wage system. Mercantilism, after all, was not hostile to individual ownership and enterprise. It merely insisted that men, while pursuing their own destinies, keep in mind the larger purposes of the sheltering state. Within those purposes there was considerable room for economic maneuver. The colonies had been founded through private initiative acting in response to national needs, and such initiative continued to power the American economy throughout the colonial period. The farmer and merchant were undoubted capitalists, and their agrarian-commerical capitalism was a plainly marked way station on the road to industrial capitalism. Although by the time of the Revolution the theory of laissez faire had become more current in England than in the colonies, the conditions favoring laissez faire were hardly less developed in the latter area.

The development of capitalist institutions in the colonies was, to be sure, a related phase of the rise of capitalism in Europe. Throughout the colonial period enterprise in America was tied in tightly to the economy of the mother country, and not until long after the great political break did England's former colonies strike out radically on their own line of economic development. If the colonies exhibited certain unique details of developing capitalism, they nevertheless conformed faithfully to the broad outlines of the European economy. As Louis Hacker has reminded us, "The growth of our economic institutionalism, that is to say, the various phases of capitalism, has been the growth of Europe's. Capitalism was a European phenomenon; and we inherited it." It does Americans no harm to remember these things, to recall, for example, that the industrial revolution in America came after and was spurred by the industrial revolution in England.

Yet the colonists made important contributions to capitalism, especially to the fact and theory of economic individualism, and thereby created an economy with a flavor all its own. The techniques and assumptions of mercantilism never did flourish as vigorously in America as in England. The state was not, and in the nature of things could not be, the bureaucratic triumph that it was in England and Europe. Mercantilism as a system of internal regulation was always in a condition of decline, although the revival of controls during the Revolution proves that its basic principles had by no means fallen into the disrepute of later times. Mercantile legislation remained on the books and mercantile assumptions in the air, but by the end of the colonial period laissez-faire practices were prevalent in commerce, manufacturing, and agriculture.

Theories of laissez faire did not keep pace with the progress of capitalism. Certain doctrines of economic individualism attained a vogue in the colonies. The common-sense creed of "industry and frugality" was proclaimed by preachers like Samuel Whitman and laymen like Franklin. There were poor boys who made good by working and saving before Ragged Dick and poor boys who made good by writing about them before Horatio Alger. A tentative belief in free trade and the profit motive persuaded the minds of several farseeing colonists. Yet a full-blown faith in laissez faire did not take hold until after the Revolution. The colonists were far more neutral in matters of economic doctrine than their ancestors or descendants. Few of them asserted for publication that this or that economic system was an absolute prerequisite of national power or human freedom. Economic thought in the colonial period was traditional, self-contradictory, primitive, and generally quite nebulous.

Whatever the state of economic theory in colonial America, economic fact pointed toward the future. The long-run trend of the colonial economy was one of expansion—in population, productivity, capital accumulation, opportunity, social mobility, goals of enterprise, and openmindedness of economic thought. An extra element of economic freedom had always been present in the American adventure. Feudal land tenure, the guild system, the efficient state, and communal agriculture had failed to take hold in the wilderness; and, once the pioneer period was past, the economy moved steadily forward under the goad of private initiative. The economic picture in 1765 had plenty of blotches—the exhaustion of soil and credit in Virginia, the growth of monopoly and land speculation, the failure to solve the currency problem, and the curse of slavery—but there can be no doubt that the American economy was, to an astounding degree, an expanding one. For all its difficulties and its organization into localized units, the American iron industry produced one-seventh of the world's supply in 1775.

III

Colonial America was divided economically into three distinct units: New England, an area of small farms and far-ranging commerce; the South, an area devoted to growing staples for export to England; and the middle colonies, an area of more conspicuous diversity and opportunity than either of the other groups of colonies.

The key economic fact about colonial New England was that it was an area fitted by nature for commerce rather than agriculture. New Hampshire, Connecticut, Rhode Island, and Massachusetts formed the most unsatisfactory group of colonies, "the most prejudicial Plantation to this Kingdom," from the English point of view, for they produced no important staple for export. The narrow and sandy coastal plain, the hills and valleys, and the boulder-strewn soil could be farmed for subsistence, but there was little incentive for growing surplus crops. Agriculture was diversified, and as elsewhere most people gained their livelihood from the soil. "Yet were the greater part of the people wholly devoted to the Plow." Among the leading products of the small farms of New England were corn, oats, barley, rye, buckwheat, fruits, vegetables, dairy products, sheep, horses, cattle, and swine. In several of these items the farmers of Massachusetts and Connecticut produced surpluses for export, especially to the West Indies, but the cash value of this trade was trifling when compared with that carried on in the staples of Virginia or the Carolinas.

Unable to rely on one or two major staples for export, yet unwilling to live without the finished goods that England alone could supply, the resourceful men of New England turned with a will to redressing the unfavorable balance of trade. Although the bulk of Northern manufactures was produced in households and other small units and was intended largely for domestic consumption, extractive industries produced surpluses for export to half the world. Fish, rum, and ships were New England's chief cashproducing exports; whale products, lumber, and to a lesser extent furs, iron, and naval stores helped swell the current of New England commerce.

The main business of New England, as the fisherman of Marblehead said, was always "to catch fish." The cod achieved sainthood in Massachusetts for perfectly sound economic reasons. Hundreds of ships and thousands of men were kept busy carrying cod to the Catholics of southern Europe (who welcomed it) and "refuse fish" to the slaves of the West Indies (who did not). Rum, the second support of New England's economic health, was manufactured in prodigious quantities. In 1774 more than sixty distilleries in Massachusetts alone produced 2,700,000 gallons from West Indian molasses and thereby contributed decisively to the success of the slave trade, the debauching of the Indians, the sustaining of patriotic morale, and the coming of the Revolution. "I know not why," John Adams wrote in 1818, "we should blush to confess that molasses was an essential ingredient in American independence." As for shipbuilding, the fact that one-third of the seven thousand-odd ships engaged in English commerce were built in American yards, most of them in the small yards of the New England coast, attests the importance of this native industry. Seventy-five per cent of all colonial commerce was carried in colonial bottoms. Shipbuilding was one American undertaking consistently smiled upon by the English authorities.

Ship, wharf, distillery, and countinghouse were the foundations of New England prosperity. Massachusetts, Rhode Island, New Hampshire, and Connecticut were the only colonies in which commerce was more important than agriculture. The coastwise trade and various triangular trades, in all of which rum was the magic potion that made the Yankee thrice welcome, poured back into New England a variety of products and forms of money that could then be shipped off to old England in payment for hardware, dry goods, small luxuries, and household furnishings. Forbidden to ship such products as fish and grains to England, the New Englanders engaged in an ocean-going commerce that seems fantastic for an essentially self-sufficient economy. The geography of New England and the compulsions of English mercantilism sent the men of Massachusetts down to the sea in ships.

The economies of Maryland, Virginia, Georgia, and the Carolinas responded more satisfactorily to the demands of mercantilism by concentrating their energies on producing a handful of staples for consumption in or reshipment by the mother country: tobacco in Maryland, Virginia, and North Carolina, rice and indigo in South Carolina and Georgia. These colonies produced other articles for export—naval stores, wheat, corn, furs, deerskins, flax, hemp, fruit, livestock, iron, and lumber—but extant statistics prove that the test of economic well-being for each colony was its ability to grow, ship, and claim a decent price for one or two staples.

The South was therefore a thoroughgoing agrarian region. Plantations dominated the economy of the tidewater; small farms flourished in the back country of Virginia and the Carolinas. Only Charleston, which in 1765 counted some five thousand white and five thousand Negro souls, could be classified as a city. Elsewhere, especially in Virginia, the configuration of the coast made it possible for many planters to load their produce aboard ships—other men's ships, of course—that came up the river to their docks. Such manufacturing or extraction as did exist—ironmaking in Maryland and Virginia, production of naval stores in the Carolinas, the activities of the ever-present sawmills and flour mills—were integrated with the main business of growing staples for export. Most articles manufactured in the South were produced and consumed on self-contained plantations.

From the outset Southern agriculture was conducted on a commercial basis. The desire of the Virginia Company for profit, the climate and soil of this area, the growing European penchant for smoking and snuffing, and the dictates of mercantilism, which could not long tolerate the outward flow of specie for Spanish tobacco, combined to make production of the "sot-weed" the consuming business of Virginia, Maryland, and North Carolina. The Southern colonies could and did grow other crops, for export as well as for home consumption: by 1750 Virginia and Maryland led all other colonies in the export of Indian corn. But it was "king tobacco" that made or broke these colonies throughout early American history. Even as late as 1770, when the urge for diversification was becoming stronger in the tobacco-producing colonies, more than one-fourth the total value of all American exports could be counted in tobacco.

The social and political results of this one-crop economy—the growth of large plantations, the amassing of fantastic debts, the creation of a landed aristocracy, the spread and consolidation of human slavery, soil exhaustion and abandonment, land speculation—are examined in other parts of this chapter or in Chapter V. My concern here is economic results: the capitalist nature of this staple-producing type of enterprise; the oversensitivity of the planter's economy to the world price of his staple; his subservience to the dictates of the mercantile system; the curse of the "invisible charges" (freight payments, commissions, interest, extremely high duties, insurance premiums, cooperage, cartage, rent), which lined the pockets of the English merchants; and the consequent existence, with little hope of redress, of an unfavorable balance of trade. Whatever prosperity seemed to exist in Virginia and Maryland was a bogus gloss over an essentially rotten economic condition. The reforms that might have corrected this situation—crop restriction, lower duties, scaling-down of debts, suppression of the slave trade, thorough changes in the marketing system—were flatly opposed by the English merchants and government. Toward the close of the colonial period many planters achieved a more healthy financial position by building up self-sufficient plantations and by branching out into other profit-making ventures, principally speculation in western lands. Yet the sway of tobacco had hardly been challenged, except by occasional writers to the press who complained of "eternal Piddling about that sovereign Weed Tobacco."

Capitalist agriculture and the plantation system were likewise characteristic of rice and indigo production in the colonies south of Virginia. Rice was first successfully cultivated at the turn of the eighteenth century. By the outbreak of the Revolution 165,000 barrels a year were moving through Charleston and Savannah, a good fraction of this total directed, by grudging permission of Parliament, to ports in Europe south of Cape Finisterre. This gave the staple-producing economies of South Carolina and Georgia an element of strength that the economies of Maryland and Virginia needed badly. Indigo was first shipped out of the southernmost colonies in the 1740's. In a few years England was taking more than one million pounds annually from Southern plantations.

All this time the back country of these colonies was filling up with men who had less capital and different ideas. The result was an expanding agrarian economy, which produced livestock, grains, naval stores, and tobacco for export, and avoided the pitfalls of the tidewater system through diversification, smaller units, and increased production for home consumption.

The region lying between Albany and Baltimore supported the best-balanced economy in colonial America. Like New England a booming commercial area, it was far less dependent on circuitous trading to pile up remittances to England. Like the South a famous agricultural belt, it grew crops less subject to price fluctuations and less destructive of the soil than the tobacco of Virginia and Maryland. Toward the middle of the eighteenth century it took the lead from New England in the number and productivity of its manufacturing enterprises. Climate, soil, topography, and ingenuity combined to make the middle colonies, especially Pennsylvania, the soundest economic unit in the imperial structure.

The expanding economy of the four middle colonies could be most readily observed in its two leading ports, Philadelphia and New York. The former served as the natural market or throat of export for Pennsylvania, Delaware, and West Jersey, the latter for East Jersey, the Hudson valley, and western Connecticut. This hinterland, like those to the north and south, was a largely self-sufficient agricultural area. Unlike that to the north, it was also able to grow large surpluses of cereals for export to southern Europe, the West Indies, New England, and even to the British Isles. Wheat, whether unprocessed or converted into flour or bread, totaled well over one-half the value of exports from both New York and Pennsylvania in the period 1760-1770.

The farms that grew this wheat and gave the region the name of "the bread colonies" were larger and more scattered than those of New England, smaller and less scattered than those to the south. Although overextended units could and did prosper with the aid of tenancy and servitude, small units were equally capable of producing wheat for the mills of the Brandywine and Raritan. In addition, the farmers of this favored region grew cattle, sheep, hogs, and horses, and shipped them or their products in the West Indies trade. Pennsylvania, New York, and Connecticut contributed a major proportion of the six thousand horses, three thousand oxen, and eighteen thousand hogs and sheep exported to the West Indies in 1770.

Whether its acres were few or many, its labor free or indentured, its crop wheat or potatoes or flax, the farm of the middle colonies was conducted on a thoroughly commercial-capitalist basis.

The growing and shipping of wheat and livestock by no means absorbed all the energies of the multinational middle colonies. Flour mills for grinding wheat, sawmills for cutting lumber, bloomeries and forges for producing and working iron, yards for building ships, and tiny factories for making paper, glass, stockings, cloth, pottery, bricks, and potash dotted the banks of rivers leading to Philadelphia or New York. In the region around Philadelphia colonial manufacturing reached its peak of development. By the middle of the eighteenth century ever-increasing amounts of surplus capital, amassed in the first instance from trade in staples, were flowing into these miniature industrial enterprises. A Swedish traveler wrote of Germantown in 1748, "Most of the inhabitants are Manufacturers, and make almost everything in such quantity and perfection, that in a short time this province will want very little from *England,* its mother country." Men lived a good life in colonial Pennsylvania, a life of liberty and prosperity, and the wonder is how few Englishmen could see how far the "real American Revolution" had run by 1765.

IV

The dominating physical feature of the American economy was the land itself. To a civilization in which land was the basis of wealth and badge of status the American colonies alone offered this treasure in abundance. Most people who came to the colonies were in search of land on which to plant and prosper. The possession of land was an absolute requirement for political participation in seven of the thirteen colonies, and everywhere it was recognized as the one indisputable "stake-in-society." If the ease with which it could be acquired, especially by well-placed officials and their favorites, released torrents of greed that made a mockery of equality, it also released the energies of tens of thousands of men who were willing to sweat for the good life.

Despite the fact of ultimate possession in the Crown and the existence of vast and often long-lived proprietary schemes, the forms and spirit of feudal tenure never took hold in America. Land was too cheap and abundant, the settlers too impatient of restrictions, England itself too advanced, and the proprietors too distant and misinformed ever to have permitted the successful transplanting of the manorial system. The bestowal of lands in "free and common socage," the most liberal grant the Crown could have made, was a decisive factor in the development of the colonies.

The enfeebling of feudalism and failure of the few attempts at communism—not to be confused with modern attempts of the same name—resulted in the triumph of private ownership as the method of landholding. Outside New England the quit rent, a fixed yearly payment to Crown or proprietor in recognition and conversion of the ancient obligations of tenantry, continued to be demanded of otherwise free and unencumbered landholders. Yet for most of those who paid quit rents the burden was small; in one famous instance the tenant's obligation was discharged by "one red rose forever." And upon those who ignored payments or fell into arrears, chiefly in New York and several proprietary colonies, retribution was rarely visited. The leading authority on quit rents has estimated "conservatively" that at the time of the Revolution the rent rolls in Crown and proprietary colonies totaled £37,500, collections £19,000.

In most colonies land could be acquired with ease

by purchase or grant. The policies of Crown, colony, and speculator alike were directed to encouraging settlement and cultivation. As the colonies became more thickly settled, unspoiled land in the older areas grew more difficult to obtain. Yet there was always the frontier, especially from Pennsylvania southward, and few were the resolute and land-hungry men who failed to acquire acres of their own. Only in ill-managed New York, where tenantry, speculation, and a manorial system flourished in unholy alliance, was it hard for the plain man to obtain land. As a result, New York lagged well behind other colonies in immigration.

This description gives too much order and simplicity to a fantastically complicated situation. The digger into land laws, deeds, and records turns up a dozen exceptions to every one rule, and the total picture often appears as one vast jumble of clouded titles, rent wars, lawsuits, feudal remnants, and cross-purposes in official policy. Yet it would be a mistake not to recognize the final sovereignty of these determinants: the failure of feudalism, the triumph of private ownership, and the ease of acquisition.

The land system of New England put simultaneous emphasis on the general purposes of the community and the special needs of the individual. The result was a pattern of landholding in Massachusetts, Connecticut, and Rhode Island, and to a lesser extent in New Hampshire, with these distinguishing features: stability of law and custom in the older settlements, orderliness in the course of westward expansion, and almost everywhere a condition of relative equality marked by small farms held in fee simple. Provisions in the various charters for tenure in free and common socage were the chief blow at feudalism, but the determination of the first New Englanders to have done with past oppressions and inequities are evident in these clauses from the Massachusetts "Body of Liberties" (1641):

10. All our lands and heritages shall be free from all fines and licenses upon Alienations, and from all hariotts, wardships, Liveries, Primer-seisins, yeare day and wast, Escheates, and forfeitures, upon the death of parents or Ancestors, be they naturall, casuall, or Juditiall.

81. When parents dye intestate, the Elder sonne shall have a doble portion of his whole estate reall and personall, unlesse the General Court upon just cause alleadged shall judge otherwise.

82. When parents dye intestate having no heires males of their bodies their daughters shall inherit as Copartners, unles the General Court upon just reason shall judge otherwise.

Thus at a stroke did Massachusetts abolish feudal obligations and primogeniture.

Most of New England was settled initially on a community basis. A group desiring to head west or north petitioned the colonial assembly for a grant of land. After the new township had been surveyed and "safety, Christian communion, schools, civility, and other good ends" had been satisfied by reserving plots for these purposes, the settlers, within certain limits, distributed the land among themselves. The amount any one man might obtain varied according to his means and needs, but rarely was gross inequality permitted by law or custom. In time the close-knit agricultural town and its system of house lots, upland fields, and commons gave way to a more dispersed, individualistic pattern. By 1750, thanks to progressive liberalization of the laws of tenure and alienation, the New England farmer was master of his own land. And by 1750, thanks to the nature of the region and the stern wisdom of the early settlers, New England was an area of small, compact farms. The eighteenth century was marred by speculation in frontier lands and by unseemly squabbles between proprietors and newcomers in some of the older settlements, but the system survived these rude shocks with comparatively little damage.

It would be wrong to point with uncritical pride to the land policies of colonial New England, for the usual abuses, frauds, quarrels, monopolies, and inequities blacken the record of even the most sensible communities. Yet enormous progress was registered in most towns toward a condition of freedom based on equality and stability. In contrast to conditions in England or even New York, the land systems of Massachusetts and Connecticut were bulwarks of human freedom.

Outside New England the various land systems were directed to economic rather than socio-religious ends. The land was generally held of the Crown or a proprietor by some form of tenure. The individual secured his own acres by purchase or grant and, especially in the latter case, was pledged to pay an annual quit rent. Since official policy favored the process of settlement, grants and sales were liberal and quit rents small. An immigrant who would actually settle down and work a piece of land generally had no trouble acquiring all he could use. Through such devices as the famous "headright" system of the Southern colonies he could get additional land by importing one or more immigrants. Moreover, he could always buy land cheaply from the government or from one of the many speculative companies that had purchased vast tracts of land or had been granted them by lazy, corrupt, or conniving authorities. In some areas he might simply strike out for himself. Squatting was a way of life among the impoverished Scotch-Irish of Pennsylvania and North Carolina, and the governments of these and several other colonies came in time to recognize this practice by law. As to authority for pre-emption, the squatters of Pennsylvania had a memorable answer:

In doing this by force, they alleged that it was against the laws of God and nature that so much land should be idle while so many Christians wanted it to labor on and to raise their bread.

The result of this laxity in the middle and Southern colonies was a system in which disorder, fraud, and inequity were more prevalent than under the New England way. Although conditions were somewhat more progressive in the middle than in the Southern colonies, engrossing and tenantry reached a peak in New York and utter confusion rock bottom in East Jersey, an area, wrote a traveling gentleman in 1744, of "so many doubtfull titles and rights that it creates an inexhaustible and profitable pool for the lawyers." Primogeniture, entails, and quit rents disappeared generally in the region south of New England only with the Revolution, although here and there—as in the case of abolition of primogeniture in Pennsylvania—more liberal techniques were adopted earlier. The quit rents provide a clear example of the way in which an economic institution can work both for and against the course of liberty. Although the quit rent was a relic of feudalism and cause of much social discontent, it was also, wherever collected with any efficiency, a powerful deterrent to large holdings and arrant speculation.

The eighteenth century witnessed a lamentable trend toward concentration in all the Southern colonies. Even in areas where the plantation held firmest sway, however, the small farmer was present in sizable numbers. The lax methods of the South had mixed social results. The conditions that made land cheaper and easier to acquire for poor men in the Carolinas than poor men in Connecticut also made possible more abuses and monopolies.

This discussion of land systems in the colonies should not end on a sour note. A shocking amount of land passed into the hands of speculators, yet

many of these people played a valuable promotional
role. It was a misfortune of the colonial period that
the thing for which the plain man hungered and
thirsted was also the thing from which returns on
capital investment were most spectacular. Yet it cannot be said that either settlement or liberty was held
back by speculation except in a few notorious instances. A gentleman in Philadelphia could report in
1768 that "Every great fortune made here within
these 50 years has been by land," but he could also
have reported that for every great fortune made by
a Quaker in Philadelphia a hundred good livings had
been made by Germans and Scotch-Irish in the valleys to the west and north. This was essentially the
state of affairs through most of colonial America. Despite a distressing catalogue of inequity, speculation,
greed, class conflict, and downright corruption, land
was easier to acquire, keep, work, sell, and will in
the colonies than in any other place in the Atlantic
world. By the middle of the eighteenth century the
land was supporting a hardy yeomanry whose children and grandchildren were to provide the spirit
and substance of the Revolution, Jeffersonian Democracy, and Jacksonian Democracy. Land for the brave
man's asking, "free land . . . open to a fit people,"
was the great gate to freedom in colonial America. Thus spoke Crèvecoeur for tens of thousands of
Americans:

The instant I enter on my own land, the bright idea of
property, of exclusive right, of independence exalt my mind.
Precious soil, I say to myself, by what singular custom of
law is it that thou wast made to constitute the riches of the
freeholder? What should we American farmers be without
the distinct possession of that soil? It feeds, it clothes us,
from it we draw even a great exuberancy, our best meat,
our richest drink, the very honey of our bees comes from
this privileged spot. No wonder we should thus cherish its
possession, no wonder that so many Europeans who have

never been able to say that such portion of land was theirs, cross the Atlantic to realise that happiness. This formerly rude soil has been converted by my father into a pleasant farm, and in return it has established all our rights; on it is founded our rank, our freedom, our power as citizens.

V

Most men in most societies work with their hands for a living. The wages and conditions of labor are therefore a reliable measure of the extent of human freedom. It was a fact of huge moment for the rise of American liberty that the price of labor was higher in the colonies than in England or Europe and that conditions of work were more humane and pleasant. Wage earners, in the modern sense of the phrase, were comparatively few in the colonies, except in certain ports, cities, and northern villages. Yet by 1765 they constituted an important class, one in which many part-time farmers could also be counted. The progress of this class toward a "democracy of labor"—a general pattern of employment marked by decent wages and working conditions, protections against arbitrary employers, a philosophy preaching the dignity of labor, opportunities for advancement, and legal cushions against disaster—gave a mighty push to American liberty. By no means were all these advantages realized, but colonial labor had come a long way from England and mercantilism.

In the mercantile system the place of labor was designedly mean and subordinate. "It was the fate of the workers to be poor that the nation might be rich," P. W. Buck writes, "and to be ceaselessly diligent that the nation might be powerful." The ideal laborer shunned idleness, raised a large family, lived in poverty, and received his pittance with a smile. The real laborer, as Defoe wrote in echo of all mercantilists, was "saucy, mutinous, and beggarly." It was therefore the business of the state to regulate him thoroughly. Maximum-wage rather than minimum-wage legislation was characteristic of mercantilism, for only by cutting labor costs to the bone could the hated "forraigners" be undersold in the struggle for markets. Government intervened in capitalist enterprise not to raise the poor man up but to keep him down.

Mercantilist doctrines of labor, which were supported at crucial points by the medieval notions of the Puritans, were brought with official approval to Massachusetts and Virginia. Most early colonies took a hard stab at legislation designed to control high wages, and the journals of the gentleman adventurers are full of complaints against "excessive rates of laborers' and workmen's wages" and "great extortion used by divers persons of little conscience." Massachusetts and her towns enacted laws and orders that set maximum wages and minimum hours, made labor compulsory under certain circumstances, punished idleness and vagrancy, and impressed certain classes for labor on public works. The other colonies were not far behind. Had the ruling class in the early colonies had its way, low wages and long hours would have been the perpetual lot of the American workingman.

The land rather than the ruling class had its way in the end. Dear land and cheap labor depressed the common man in Europe; cheap land and dear labor raised him up in America. The existence of vast tracts of land and of schemes for their settlement drew a constant stream of workers away from wage-earning and into agricultural self-support. The economic history of the colonies is marked by a chronic scarcity of all types of labor and thus by a consistently high scale of wages. Mercantilism and medievalism alike were undermined by the American environment. Regulation of wages and of other problems of labor was gradually abandoned, first by the colonies, then by the towns. A great mass of early legislation went unenforced, and further attempts at regulation were discouraged. Dozens of diaries and official reports pay tribute to the lure of uncultivated lands. Governor John Wentworth of New Hampshire wrote in 1768:

> The people are by no means inclined to any sort of manufacture. Scarcely a shoemaker, a joiner, or silversmith but quits his trade, as soon as he can get able to buy a little tract of land and build a cottage in the wilderness.

Governor Henry Moore of New York echoed this observation in a letter to the Board of Trade (1767):

> The Price of Labour is so great in this part of the World, that it will always prove the greatest obstacle to any Manufactures attempted to be set up here, and the genius of the People in a Country where every one can have Land to work upon leads them so naturally into Agriculture, that it prevails over every other occupation.

The author of *American Husbandry* (1775) spoke of the paradoxical fact that "nothing but a high price will induce men to labour at all, and at the same time it presently puts a conclusion to it by so soon enabling them to take a piece of waste land." Other factors, too, such as the cost of transportation from Europe, kept wages high.

The result was, as William Penn testified, that America was "a good poor Man's country." Not only were nominal wages two or three times those prevalent in England, but real wages, according to Richard B. Morris, "exceeded by 30 to 100 per cent the wages of a contemporary English workman." The differences between colonial and English wages became less pronounced in the eighteenth century, but the real price of labor was always higher in the colonies. The Royal Navy had to be especially on guard against desertion from ships in colonial ports. From Hell to Paradise was a short swim.

As wages were higher, so were conditions of work better. The laborer, who knew as well as his master of the existence of cheap land, must certainly have been a freer spirit than his hemmed-in British brother. Part-time subsistence agriculture gave thousands of wage earners an added measure of security. The absence of any remnants of the guild system gave other men the security that goes with being a jack-of-all-trades. "If any one could or would carry on ten trades," wrote a German traveler, "no one would have a right to prevent him." And apparently many colonists did carry on at least a half-dozen at a time. Even the apprentice system seems to have been more easygoing, since it was often directed to purposes other than the maintenance of craft traditions and monopolies.

In our terms, of course, conditions of labor were hard and primitive. The great panoply of protective legislation that cushions the shock of industrial capitalism had only a meager counterpart in colonial statutes. No unions emerged to give the colonial worker the strength of collectivity. No strike of workingmen took place in the colonial era. No laborsaving machinery was installed on a large scale—to be welcomed or resisted. The worker in America, as everywhere in the Western world, had to shift for himself. Yet it could be said of America, as of nowhere in the Western world, that cheap land, high wages, short supply, and increasing social mobility permitted the worker to shift for himself with some hope of success. By our standards his life was "poore, nasty, brutish, and short." By the standards of seventeenth- and eighteenth-century England or Germany his life was free and productive.

The high price of labor had ill effects as well as good. An abundance of land and a scarcity of free labor drove profit-seeking planters and farmers to the easy but unhappy solution of unfree labor. Whatever the price or quantity of free labor, slavery and the indenture system would have developed in the colonies; yet the thriving condition of slavery in the South and of bonded servitude in the middle colonies was nourished by the dearness of free labor. The indenture system was, all things considered, a useful solution to one of the hard problems of a new country in a rough age, but slavery was a curse for which we have not yet paid the full price. If the colonial system of labor made many men free, it made other men slaves or, what is often worse, slaveowners. And in the end it was the skilled white artisan who suffered as much as anyone in the South, for the slave artisan replaced him almost completely in rural areas.

In New England and the middle colonies the rise of a sizable body of skilled and unskilled free workers was a boon to political liberty. The colonial craftsman, as Carl Bridenbaugh has demonstrated, was a far more reputable person socially and politically than his counterpart in England. Urban craftsmen were among the prime movers in the events of 1765 and 1775. The unskilled laborer, though still disfranchised, found his public voice in these headstrong years. The relative absence of poverty in the colonies had helped create a lower class ready for political emancipation. The Revolution did not free this class completely, but it stirred it to considerable activity.

VI

The seeds of independence were planted deep in "the old colonial system"—a relationship in which one country assumed the role of eternal master over another that was peopled with some of its best stock and blessed with limitless opportunities for expansion. Englishmen in the American environment, and men of other proud breeds as well, would not always be satisfied with the short end of mercantilism. Few colonial writers echoed the elaborate mercantilist justification of colonies by remarking how pleasant it would be to remain forever a source of raw materials and market for finished goods.

The old colonial system was not just a figment of the ripe imaginations of Daniel Defoe, John Cary, Malachy Postlethwayt, and Sir Josiah Child. It existed in fact as well as theory—most concretely in the enforcement of the celebrated Navigation Acts, which governed England's commercial policy from 1651 to 1849. Of the three hundred-odd instances of commercial legislation enacted in these two centuries, three laws in particular were directed toward the colonies: the Navigation Act of 1660 (re-enacted in 1661), the Staple Act of 1663, and the Act of Frauds of 1696. For the colonies these laws laid down three controlling principles: (1) Trade between Britain and the colonies was barred to all but English or colonial ships manned by crews three-fourths Englishmen or colonists. (2) All colonial imports from Europe, except wine and salt from southern Europe (and before the Act of Union of 1707 servants, horses, and provisions from Scotland), had to pass through England. (3) Many colonial products were placed on the "enumerated" list—including, at one time or another, tobacco, sugar, indigo, rice, cotton, molasses, naval stores, spices, dye woods, pig iron and bar iron, potash, hides, whale fins, and numerous other commodities England could not produce herself. These articles could be exported by the colonies only to Britain, Ireland, or other English colonies.

The Navigation Acts and their many modifications were plainly designed for mercantile ends. Through them England intended to secure a monopoly of the trade of the colonies: to take from them, at her own price, whatever colonial products she needed; to ship them, again at her own price, surpluses of finished goods; and to make sizable additional profits by acting as the mandatory entrepôt for colonial exports to and imports from Europe. At the same time, the colonists were left free to trade with the West Indies and southern Europe in such products as flour and fish, in order to pile up specie and credits to pay for still more English wares.

These acts guaranteed to English merchants the richest fruits of colonial commerce. The bounty system and other favoring legislation spurred the production of needed raw materials and staples. The only remaining problem for mercantilist concern was the potential threat of colonial manufacturing. The English manufacturers persuaded Parliament to meet this threat with three isolated but thoroughly imperial statutes: the Woolens Act of 1699, the Hat Act of 1732, and the Iron Act of 1750. Each of these was designed to frustrate the growth of a colonial industry that was threatening to poach on the privileged preserve of a group of English manufacturers. The Woolens Act forbade the export of wool and wool products from one colony to another or to a foreign country. The Hat Act forbade the export of hats and limited each hatmaker to two apprentices. The Iron Act forbade the erection of ironworking establishments, and at the same time removed all duties on colonial pig iron and bar iron shipped to England. One final statute aimed at the overweening colonists was the result of the pressures of a uniquely vested interest. The Molasses Act of 1733, which imposed prohibitive duties on rum, molasses, and sugar imported into the colonies from the non-British West Indies, was passed by Parliament under the whip of an organized minority. In the French West Indies the Northern merchants had found a cheaper, more plentiful source of raw materials for New England rum, and the planters of the sugar islands—many of whom lived in England and sat in Parliament—were determined to ruin the French even if this meant ruining the New Englanders as well.

More important than the laws themselves was the manner of their enforcement. Generations of historians have sought to evaluate the administration of this array of legislation, and on these points general agreement now exists: The Navigation Acts were, all things considered, reasonably well enforced, especially after the Act of 1696 incorporating governors in the administrative system and orders of 1697 standardizing procedures for vice-admiralty courts. The Woolens, Hat, and Iron acts were largely ignored by the colonists, since machinery for steady enforcement of this program did not exist. The Molasses Act, as every schoolboy knows or used to know, was the most flagrantly disregarded law between the Seventh Commandment and the Volstead Act. The Molasses Act, not the Navigation Acts, made smuggling part of the early American way of life. The extent of this practice is indicated in the fact that Rhode Island alone imported more molasses annually than the total output of the British West Indies. So vital was this trade to the commercial colonies that it persisted throughout the French and Indian War— an act of treason on an epic scale. In an average year in the 1750's Massachusetts merchants imported 500 hogsheads of molasses legally from the British West Indies and 14,500 hogsheads illegally from the French. This made for a lot of headaches in New England as well as old.

The Privy Council, spurred and supported by the Board of Trade, did its part to keep the colonies in their proper place in the old colonial system. It disallowed provincial laws that encouraged home industries, discriminated against English wares, scaled down the eternal and ever-mounting colonial debts, placed export duties on enumerated commodities or import duties on English merchandise, monopolized Indian trade, authorized payments of quit rents in paper money, interfered with the transporting of convicts and slaves, or in any way smacked of possible independence rather than perpetual dependence. Specific and circular instructions went out to governors advising them to exercise this or that power, especially the veto, for mercantile ends. Parliament was advised of the need for legislation to check colonial presumptions. In such defenses of the old colonial system as the fight against paper money, the Privy Council used all these methods—disallowance, instructions, and legislative recommendations—with vigor and success.

The economic results of this network of law and administration were not nearly so disastrous as some historians have insisted. L. A. Harper has estimated tentatively that the burdens of mercantilism cost the colonies something over three million dollars a year. An example of how English merchants reaped extra profits from the system is the fact that in the 1760's they re-exported three-fourths of the tobacco and rice imported from the Southern colonies. Yet Harper is quick to point out that the imperial blessings of military and naval protection cannot be reckoned in statistical tables. Certainly the colonies received many benefits, the most important of which was their qualified inclusion in, rather than total exclusion from, a great commercial system. England was the natural monopolist of much of the colonists' trade and looked with favor, or at worst with neutrality, on much of the circuitous trade based on fish, flour, provisions, and rum. Although the Woolens, Hat, and Iron acts may have frightened some timid capital away from these infant enterprises, colonial conditions rather than English laws explain the absence of manufacturing. The industrial development of the colonies was just about where it would have been had Americans been allowed to determine their own policies. Until the middle of the eighteenth century colonial and world conditions were such that the Americans, especially the merchants of the North, gained more than they lost from the old colonial system.

The political results of mercantilism were favorable to the growth of liberty and self-government. For all their benefits to the colonies, the Navigation Acts were a constant source of petty irritation to many colonial merchants, farmers, and consumers, causing them, as a Swedish traveler noted in 1748, "to grow less tender for their mother country." The tension that existed between colonial and vice-admiralty courts was one major cause and effect of this irritation. The Woolens and Hat acts stirred up few political quarrels, but the Iron Act, which was aimed at the fastest-growing and most menacing colonial industry, was followed in due course by provincial laws encouraging new plants in New Jersey, Massachusetts, and Pennsylvania. The Iron Act was far more helpful to colonial propagandists than it was harmful to colonial merchants. The employment of gubernatorial veto and royal disallowance to slap down headstrong colonial legislation on subjects such as land, currency, and commerce evoked considerable protest. A large proportion of the political battles between governor and assembly were fought over economic problems. For example, behind the political squabbles over paper money stood the opposing economic camps of hard-money England and easy-money America. The Paper Money Act of 1751 was a portent of things to come. Most merchants begged for it; the rural debtors opposed it. Between them they managed to raise for the first time in years the question of Parliament's authority. The clash of colonial aspiration and imperial mercantilism was a constant spur to republicanism in thought and action.

After 1765, of course, the conflict of English and American economic self-interest became more intense and sharply defined. It is not my business to weigh again, as so many historians have weighed, the many causes of the American Revolution. It should be sufficient to remark that for one compelling economic reason—the rise of the colonies to a level of population, ingenuity, and surplus capital at which the growth of economic independence was about to begin—the determination of George III's government to tighten up the loose stays in the old colonial system was certain to lead to political trouble. The further determination of his government to restrict the few allowable outlets for colonial capital and initiative—western lands and ocean-going commerce—did as much to hasten the final breach as did any other factor. Yet this book is the story of colonial development before 1765, and in this period economic forces helped create only the first of the two revolutions necessary for independence. Soil, sea, and forest; commerce, agriculture, and manufacturing; free labor, servitude, and slavery; countinghouse, mill, farm, and plantation; rum, tobacco, rice, and flour; private ownership, profits, speculation, wages, and credits; and above all the growth of economic opportunity, mobility, and individualism—these were the marks, not all of them exactly inspiring, of an economy that could not go on much longer in a state of political dependency. The wisest English heads were already convinced that the colonies, especially those to the north, "in respect of climate, soil, agriculture and manufactures, possess most of the requisites of an independant people." Burke caught the flavor of American enterprise when he paid his famous tribute to the New England whalers:

Whilst we follow them among the tumbling mountains of ice, and behold them penetrating into the deepest frozen recesses of Hudson's Bay and Davis's Straits, whilst we are looking for them beneath the arctic circle, we hear that they have pierced into the opposite region of polar cold, that they are at the antipodes, and engaged under the frozen serpent of the south. Falkland Island, which seemed too remote and romantic an object for the grasp of national ambition, is but a stage and resting-place in the progress of their victorious industry. Nor is the equinoctial heat more discouraging to them, than the accumulated winter of both the poles. We know that whilst some of them draw the line and strike the harpoon on the coast of Africa, others run the longitude, and pursue their gigantic game along the coast of Brazil. No sea but what is vexed by their fisheries. No climate that is not witness to their toils.

Such a people, it seems plain, were no longer colonists, to be regulated and taxed for the benefit of others.

III

The Dissidence of Dissent: Religion in the Colonies

—————◆◎◆—————

The influence of religion on government has always been profound. If it is dangerous to frame general laws about this influence, especially to insist that authoritarianism or democracy or anarchy in church leads to authoritarianism or democracy or anarchy in state, it is equally dangerous not to acknowledge that at certain times in certain countries the consequences of religion for politics have been earth-shaking.

One thing is sure about church and state in the Atlantic community, and history does not teach a more emphatic lesson: The great struggles for religious liberty, whatever the motivations of each group or individual taking part in them, contributed directly to the rise of political liberty.

The Western world . . . as we live in it and think it, was really forged in the clash of warring sects and opinions, in the secular feuds between the clergy and laity, Catholic and Protestant, Lutheran and Calvinist. . . . It is not too much to say that political liberty would not now-a-days exist anywhere but for the claim to ecclesiastical independence.

If this claim of Father Figgis is too sweeping for secular minds, we have Harold Laski's opinion that "the political liberty of the seventeenth and eighteenth centuries was the outcome of the protest against religious intolerance." It is hard to escape the conclusion that political democracy flourished first, and flourishes most vigorously today, in those countries where religion has been most tolerant and humane. The free state rests squarely, both logically and historically, on freedom of religion.

The rise of political liberty in colonial America is an exciting testament to this noble truth. The unending struggles for toleration, disestablishment, and liberty of profession were one of the most powerful human-directed forces working for individual freedom and constitutional government. The establishment of religious freedom was no less momentous an achievement than the clearing of the great forest or the winning of independence, for the twin doctrines of separation of church and state and liberty of individual conscience are the marrow of our democracy, if not indeed America's most magnificent contribution to the freeing of Western man.

I

The pattern of religion in colonial America was diversified and shifting, varying significantly and often sharply from one colony to another and from one decade to the next. From the welter of complexity and detail these salient features loom up:

An overwhelming proportion of the colonists was Protestant in persuasion or background. Catholics, except for short seasons in scattered locations, were feared, despised, slandered, and "warned out," not least, as one colonial penman put it, because "Popery is a great Friend to *arbitrary Government*." The wars with France and Spain and the Pretender's rebellion of 1746 strengthened the colonist's loathing of the "Papist." Throughout most of the colonial period— "The Penal Period," as Catholic historians label it— every colony carried anti-Catholic legislation on its books.

It should never be forgotten, even or especially in an age of economic determinism, that religion was a leading motive in some of the most important explorations and settlements. Several colonies were established as havens for the oppressed of one faith, several others as havens for the oppressed of all, still others as economic ventures in which toleration of dissenting consciences was encouraged as "good for business"; and throughout the colonial period the Protestant assault on Roman Catholicism was a prime reason for settling and defending the American colonies. Any interpretation of early American history that ignores religious motivation is essentially unsound.

The English origin of the early colonists was the deciding factor in the relations of church and state in most colonies. The men of Virginia, the Carolinas, and Massachusetts had come from a country where the union of church and state, with the latter the dominant partner, was an accepted part of the way of life. It should therefore occasion no surprise to learn that in nine of the thirteen colonies a state church was established and maintained in the colonial period—the Anglican Church in Virginia, Maryland (after 1702), the Carolinas, Georgia, and the southern counties of New York; the Congregational Church in Massachusetts (as well as Plymouth), Connecticut (as well as New Haven), and the towns of New Hampshire. No church was ever established in Rhode Island, Pennsylvania, or Delaware, nor, after the coming of the English, in New Jersey. Despite the growth of dissent and toleration, despite the fact that in several colonies the established Anglican Church claimed only a fraction of the inhabitants, nine colonies went into the Revolution with religious privilege fixed in law and charter. The dissolving of the political bands that had connected them with a superior power brought an end to establishment in most of the new states.

Eighteenth-century America was the world's warmest nursery of sects and sectarians. The most reliable census of early American churches and congregations lists these figures for 1775: Congregational, 668; Presbyterian, 588; Anglican, 495; Baptist, 494; Quaker, 310; German Reformed, 159; Lutheran, 150; Dutch Reformed, 120; Methodist, 65; Catholic, 56; Moravian, 31; Congregational-Separatist, 27; Dunker, 24; Mennonite, 16; French Protestant, 7; Sandemanian, 6; Jewish, 5; Rogerene, 3—a catalogue that could be rendered even more motley by calling attention to severe doctrinal conflicts in several of these groupings, for example, between "New Lights" and "Old Lights" in Connecticut Congregationalism and between "New Sides" and "Old Sides" in Virginia Presbyterianism. A study of Pennsylvania in 1776 gives this count of churches in the dissenters' paradise: German Reformed, 106; Presbyterian, 68; Lutheran, 63; Quaker, 61; Anglican, 33; Baptist, 27; Moravian, 14; Mennonite, 13; Dunker, 13; Catholic, 9; Dutch Reformed, 1. Even in seventeenth-century Massachusetts unity of doctrine was more apparent than real. As to the eighteenth century, when the splintering effects of Protestantism and the American environment had done their worst (or best), one town in Massachusetts is reported to have harbored six mutually independent Baptist churches. Which of them had God's ear is not made clear in the report.

Despite this network of highways to Heaven, or turnpikes to Tophet, an astounding number of colonists belonged to no church at all. One reason was the poverty of such colonies as North Carolina and of such colonists as the early Germans and Scotch-Irish in Pennsylvania. Another was the fact that church membership in all colonies was a matter of individual choice, and that religion was therefore personalized rather than institutionalized. A third reason was the casual attitude toward religion prevalent, for quite different reasons, in both the lowest and highest strata of colonial society. By the middle of the eighteenth century there was a larger percentage of "non-professing Christians" in the American colonies than in any state in Western Europe.

Throughout the colonial period—amid scenes of establishment and disestablishment, struggle and brotherhood, persecution and toleration, decline and revival, consecration and indifference—the course of American religion moved ever away from feudalism and onward toward modern times. The line from John Cotton to Jonathan Mayhew extends from one pole of Puritanism to the other, yet it is astonishingly direct and easily followed. Under the pressure of the American environment Christianity grew more humanistic and temperate—more tolerant with the struggle of the sects, more liberal with the growth of optimism and rationalism, more experimental with the rise of science, more individualistic with the advent of democracy. Equally important, increasing numbers of colonists, as a legion of preachers loudly lamented, were turning secular in curiosity and skeptical in attitude. They might still believe, but their theology had softened, their sense of sin had disappeared, and their thoughts were of performance in this world rather than of salvation in the other. The violence of the Great Awakening was a lefthanded tribute to the sweep of this trend. "That old-time religion" was a far less potent element in colonial life in 1765 than it had been in 1630, 1675, or even 1700.

II

Out of all these forces and trends three conditions were working most powerfully for political and social liberty: the spirit and institutions of Protestantism; the multiplicity of religions; and the increasing proportion of the unchurched, worldly, and indifferent. These three factors in turn helped create a fourth, the struggle for religious liberty, and this factor did as much as all the others combined to bring about the "real American Revolution."

Burke caught the spirit of American religion in words that could not conceivably be improved upon:

The people are Protestants; and of that kind which is the most adverse to all implicit submission of mind and opinion. This is a persuasion not only favourable to liberty, but built upon it. . . . The dissenting interests have sprung up in direct opposition to all the ordinary powers of the world; and could justify that opposition only on a strong claim to natural liberty. Their very existence depended on the powerful and unremitted assertion of that claim. All Protestantism, even the most cold and passive, is a sort of dissent. But the religion most prevalent in our northern colonies is a refinement on the principle of resistance; it is the dissidence of dissent, and the Protestantism of the Protestant religion.

Dissent and resistance, the effective impulses of American Protestantism in the seventeenth and eighteenth centuries, have always been first causes of religious freedom. Yet the Protestant strain spurred the growth of liberty in other ways. Church government in the colonies, which even in Anglican Virginia emphasized the self-directing competence of the congregation at the expense of hierarchy, helped democratize political organization. The belief in an infallible Bible advertised the glories of higher law; Locke rode into New England on the backs of Moses and the prophets. At the same time, the Old Testament was a channel through which some of the liberating doctrines of the Hebraic tradition were fed into the American stream. And the concept of the chosen people, which was as strong in seventeenth-century Boston as it had been in ancient Israel, was to prove easily convertible—by such men as Mayhew,

Edwards, John Adams, Washington, and Jefferson—into the noble democratic doctrine of the American Mission.

American democracy owes its greatest debt to colonial Protestantism for the momentum it gave to the growth of individualism. The Reformation, which was powered by the revolutionary notion that man could commune with God without the intercession of a priest, did as much as the rise of capitalism to spread the doctrine of individualism. As the Protestants of Protestantism, the dissidents of dissent, the men of the American churches stressed the salvation of the individual rather than the maintenance of communal unity or doctrinal purity. Calvinist in inspiration and Puritan in essence, the great dissenting churches helped breed a new person, and this man, multiplied millions of times over, was to give American democracy its peculiar flavor. In its best aspects and moments Protestantism was a main source of these great principles of American democracy: freedom of thought and expression, separation of church and state, local self-government, higher law, constitutionalism, the American Mission, and the free individual.

Even in its worst aspects and moments, of which there were many, Protestantism in America seemed intent on making certain a democratic future. The seasons of persecution and intolerance, in which the New England churches engaged most deplorably, only hastened the seasons of brotherhood and indifference. At least one reason for the strength of the American doctrine of religious liberty is the fact that men not only had to flee persecution in Europe but had to fight it in America. The Puritans did their grim part for religious liberty when they hanged Mary Dyer. It may be a case of having one's cake and eating it, too, to argue that oppression did as much as toleration to lead the colonies to more humane and liberal religion. Yet it is hard to suppress the feeling that the stern Puritans—and the superior Anglicans, too—were necessary actors in the great drama of religious liberty.

The pattern of religious diversity in colonial America has already been described in actual figures. This amazing variety, the delight or despair of dozens of articulate European visitors, aided the growth of liberty in several ways. First, it is a commonplace that diversity—sectional, economic, racial, religious —has been the sign, strength, and test of American democracy. The earliest of our diversities was in religious belief and practice. The central religious problem of colonial America was to create an environment in which men of differing faiths could live together in peace. The fact that such an environment was created seems all the more remarkable when we remember that dissent and treason were still synonymous in much of the Christian world. The pluralistic nature of American society may be traced in part to the multiple pattern of colonial faith.

The American tendency to splinter into sects over fine points of doctrine and worship carried the spirit of Protestantism to its logical conclusion. If the right of private judgment was achieved at the expense of a sense of community, if the hopes of one great Christian edifice were smashed into the rubble of a hundred raucous creeds, the Protestant ethic had none the less been fulfilled. Nowhere in the eighteenth-century world, with one or two possible exceptions, did the Protestant urge to protest have freer play. Nowhere was the impact of Protestantism more destructive of medieval notions of man, society, church, and God.

The rapid multiplication of the sects made toleration, and in time religious liberty, a social necessity. The doctrine of political equality of faiths was not the result of sweet reasoning about the brotherhood of man, but of the plain necessity that each sect in order to live had also to let live. A child of necessity, too, was the doctrine of separation of church and state. Even the religions that insisted most vociferously on their exclusive claims to truth contributed to this liberalizing process. The Catholic in seventeenth-century Maryland and the Anglican in eighteenth-century Massachusetts plumped as hard as any Baptist for religious freedom, not out of conviction but in the interests of self-preservation.

Finally, the increasing variety of religious beliefs, especially in the middle colonies and certain areas in the South, accustomed colonists to live on mutually respectful if not loving terms with men whose creeds were different from their own. The fact of religious diversity taught individuals as well as governments the practical advantages of toleration and religious liberty. A man who does business, especially profitable business, with all sorts of heretics may come in time to suspect that they are not heretics at all.

A factor of immense importance for the rise of liberty in America was the half-forgotten truth that large numbers of colonists took no part at all in the religious life of their communities. Some of these people were "unchurched" in the physical sense: They could not have gone to church or asked counsel of a minister even had they wanted to. An eyewitness account of religious life in the Carolinas in the early eighteenth century had this to say:

This is *South-Carolina*, extending in Length on the Sea-Coast, 300 Miles; and into the main Land near 200 Miles. It was granted by Patent from the Crown, in the Year 1663, and settled soon after, containing in the Year 1701, above 7000 Persons, besides *Negroes* and Indians, and was divided into several Parishes and Towns. Yet tho' peopled at its first Settlement with the Natives of these Kingdoms, there was, until the Year 1701, no Minister of the Church of *England* Resident in this Colony; tho' great Numbers of

the Inhabitants were very desirous of having Ministers of
the Church of *England*. . . .

The next Colony, *North-Carolina*, extending on the Sea-
Coast above 100 Miles, and into the Land about 100, was
divided into several Townships, and peopled from *England*.
It contained above 5000 Inhabitants, besides *Negroes* and
Indians, in the Year 1701, all living without any Form of
Divine Worship publickly performed.

And in 1729 Colonel Byrd wrote of the capital of
North Carolina:

I believe this is the only Metropolis in the Christian or
Mahometan World, where there is neither Church, Chappel,
Mosque, Synagogue, or any other place of Publick Wor-
ship of any Sect or Religion whatsoever.

Throughout the colonial period people in many
areas were simply too poor to support even the lowest grade of minister, especially if their doctrinal differences made it impossible to unite in one church.
Many colonists had come from the lower economic
classes in England and Germany. In the old countries
their attachment to the church had been nominal; in
the new they lost contact completely. The struggle
for existence had much to do with the unchurching
of the poor.

A second group that carried on quite oblivious of
organized religion was composed of people more toward the middle or even the upper end of the social
scale. The attitudes of secularism, of concern with
one world at a time and even disbelief in any other,
appealed to thousands of colonists whose fathers had
been stout believers in the finer shadings of doctrine. Governor Dongan of New York, himself a liberal Catholic, testified to the presence of such people
in his province in 1687:

New York has first a Chaplain belonging to the Fort of
the Church of England; secondly a Dutch Calvinist, thirdly
a French Calvinist; fourthly a Dutch Lutheran—Here bee

not many of the Church of England; few Roman Catholicks; abundance of Quakers preachers men and women especially; Singing Quakers; Ranting Quakers; Sabbatarians; Antisabbatarians; some Anabaptists some Independants; some Jews; in short of all sorts of opinion there are some, and the most part, of none at all.

Even then New York was a haven for those whose religion was "none at all," but in other colonies, too, the early fervor was on the wane. The rantings of the later Mathers and the explosiveness of the Great Awakening show how far the worldly attitude had penetrated even orthodox Massachusetts. Religion cooled off in eighteenth-century America, and a dozen awakenings would not have got the old fires going again.

A third group was made up of those who were outside any church not by compulsion or carelessness but by design. Uniquely privileged to choose between taking their religion or leaving it alone, thousands of colonists chose the second alternative. Men of this description—Franklin, John Adams, and Jefferson were typical—were not so much indifferent to religion as they were to religions. Some were rationalists, some deists; some were completely unchurched, others nominal adherents but actual nonparticipants. Most proclaimed their allegiance to the person and teachings of Jesus, but for them he was not much more than a magnificent moralist. Most, being practical men, supported the churches as aids to ordered liberty. The deists and rationalists, and there were ministers among them, were two more sects for sectarian America. The Masons, too, must be included in this reckoning.

All these men—the frontier farmer in his harsh poverty, the tavernkeeper in his worldly apathy, the merchant in his rationalized indifference—were foes of establishment, tithes, intolerance, and doctrinal dispute. To them as much as to any group we owe our state without a church. An entire nation of them would have been a calamity for stability and freedom, but as a third or fourth of a nation they were unwitting workers for liberty. Again we are having our cake and relishing it, too, but history teaches that irreligion, taken in moderate doses, has helped more than one body politic to win religious and social liberty.

III

Had religious freedom existed from the outset in all colonies, it could hardly have been so vigorous an ingredient in the rise of American liberty. But the fact that nine of thirteen colonies sooner or later set up a state church, and that only in Rhode Island was genuine religious liberty established at the beginning and maintained through the years, makes clear that whatever freedom existed in 1765 was the harvest of a long season of growth. The winning of religious liberty can be understood partly in terms of tension and conflict, partly in terms of silent, almost unnoticed development. A mass of social and economic pressures was working for freedom of religion, a mass of memory and vested interests against it. One result was struggle, and the result of struggle was liberty, not only in the religious, but also in the social, economic, and political phases of colonial life.

From the beginning it was plain to men in each colony that the fight against religious autocracy was likewise a fight against political autocracy. In Puritan Massachusetts, where until 1691 a man could not vote unless he had been admitted to the one church in town, any blow struck for religious liberty was struck just as hard for political liberty. In Anglican Virginia, where the royal governor headed the established church, the campaign for toleration was always regarded as a form of political subversion. Said Governor Gooch of certain Presbyterians who were trying his patience, "It is not liberty of conscience, but freedom of speech, they so earnestly prosecute," which was doubtless true. Freedom of speech, representation, constitutionalism, official responsibility, the suffrage, and the prized colonial right to be left alone and not taxed for other men's interests (especially for the support of their clergy)—all these principles of political liberty were invigorated by the arguments and techniques of the dissenting churches. At the same time, the men who would not be stilled, above all Quaker and Baptist, got more support than they realized from the ever-increasing multitude that dissented in silence.

It would hardly be profitable to trace the ups and downs of religious freedom in each of the colonies. In those where nonconformity came hardest, and thus where the struggle had the most influence on politics, the area of religious freedom was increased by painful steps. Toleration rather than separation was the immediate goal of Quaker in Massachusetts, Anglican in Connecticut, Presbyterian in Virginia, and Catholic everywhere. The actual achievements of colonial America were toleration in all colonies, disestablishment in four of them, and the creation of a full-bodied philosophy of religious liberty that triumphed at last during and after the Revolution. Hardly less important was the spread of a general spirit of live-and-let-live, worship-and-let-worship, which meant, for example, that dozens of severe laws punishing all manner of alleged heresies were rarely enforced in the eighteenth century. If Pennsylvanians are reminded that the Charter of Privileges of 1701 limited residence to those who believed in God, and political activity to those who believed in "*Jesus Christ*, the Saviour of the World," they may answer that there is no instance on record of the application of these restrictions, not even in the case of Benjamin Franklin.

The circumstances that made possible the victory over religious privilege are an especially satisfying example of the interplay of ethics and environment. I have already noted three of these circumstances: Protestantism, multiplicity of religions, and the great unchurched. These were the fundamental reasons for the absence in almost every colony of a recognizable religious majority, and thus for the growth of an awareness that any other course but toleration, and in time separation, would be inexpedient if not impossible to follow. Most colonials had a minority attitude toward relations of church and state, and the core of this attitude could have been no other than the "permission of dissenting consciences."

A fourth influence for religious liberty in the colonies was English practice and persuasion. Although the main pressure from England was for Anglican uniformity, and although the mother country lagged behind many of her colonies in progress toward religious freedom, Englishmen helped the cause of dissent in several ways. Proprietors and stockholders in many of the first settlements realized that some measure of toleration was necessary to induce colonists to hazard their fortunes in the new world. Even so orthodox a monarch as Charles II approved charters with liberty-of-conscience clauses in the interest of imperial prosperity. The Board of Trade warned Virginia in 1752 not to persecute dissenters, for "Toleration and a free Exercise of Religion" were "essential to the enriching and improving of a Trading Nation." And in 1704 the King-in-Council disallowed two Maryland anti-Catholic laws as tending "to depopulate that profitable colony." Other English influences for religious liberty were important—for example, the large measure of freedom granted out of principle rather than expediency by proprietors like William Penn and the Earl of Shaftesbury, the political pressure exerted by Quakers in England for royal intervention in behalf of persecuted colleagues in Massachusetts, and the extension of the Act of Toleration of 1689 to several colonies. The commercial motive, however, was the most influential.

Many colonial leaders shared this experience-proved opinion that oppression and persecution were bad for business. Indeed, most of them were convinced that a policy of government noninterference in religious affairs was an essential not only of commercial prosperity but of survival itself. The arguments from expediency of the leaders of commerce were some of the heaviest guns in the campaign for religious liberty. The most perceptive colonists had a clear idea of the distance religious liberty had traveled, the distance it had yet to go, and the welcome results for free government that the final victory would secure. They saw that the course of religious liberty was doubly important for such government —important for the political liberties it dragged in its wake, important because religious liberty was itself a political liberty. Their own experience and the history of England and Europe told them that the union of church and state was an inherently autocratic arrangement, and that those who achieved religious freedom were about two-thirds of the way to political and social freedom as well. They believed with a famous North Carolina radical: "It is a most certain fact . . . that the blending of civil and religious offices, sacred and secular things, has been an introduction to slavery in all nations where arbitrary government has been introduced."

The example of such experiments as Rhode Island and the Quaker colonies was a potent force for freedom. Biographers of Williams and Penn have claimed too much for Rhode Island and Pennsylvania, forgetting that the struggle for religious liberty had to go forward in thirteen separate and often isolated salients. Yet the success of the free colonies, advertised through the growing network of intercolonial contacts, did teach men in Massachusetts, Virginia, Maryland, and New York that religious freedom was a support rather than a subversion of political and social stability.

Yet another reason was the gospel of freedom preached and practiced by those individuals, such as Roger Williams and John Clarke, and those sects, notably Baptists and Quakers, who believed in religious liberty as a matter of principle. Most Protestant groups argued for toleration or liberty out of sheer expediency—because they were a hunted minority in an intolerant colony or were weary of sectarian disputes or were sensible enough to see the impossibility of achieving meaningful unity in a situation of hopeless diversity. A few brave men, however, made their contribution to the liberty of later generations directly rather than accidentally. American religious liberty has its fair share of prophets, philosophers, saints, and martyrs.

It is hard to overstate the political importance of pioneers in religious liberty like Williams, Clarke, Calvert, Penn, and Davies, for the devotion of these eminent men and of their thousands of co-workers helped smooth the course of government in the future republic. By demanding that the state cease supporting one religion at the expense of all, they helped return government to its proper sphere of operation. By encouraging men of one religion to show respect for men of other religions, they brought light and reason to political as well as religious controversy. By attacking religious intolerance without attacking religion, they brought the vast majority of America's churches to the side of politi-

cal liberty. And in insisting that each church stand
on its own feet without secular support, they puri-
fied and strengthened religion itself. We may return
thanks to them, not only for our tradition of religious liberty, but for a politics in which religion is
still wisely considered an alien intruder.

A final ingredient of religious liberty was the
struggle for self-government. This account has
stressed the historical and logical influence of religion
on politics, but the reverse of this process might also
have been argued. The reform elements in colonial
America—levelers, radical Whigs, republicans, and
just plain troublemakers—were all opponents of the
powerful state. In their attacks on arbitrary power,
even when their only purpose was to grasp a little
power for themselves, they undercut the dominance
of state over church. Wherever political and religious
oligarchy went hand in hand, an assault on the former, even for the most secular purposes, was sure to
be an assault on the latter. Particularly in Massachusetts did the attempt to wrest power from the magistrates weaken the position of the ministers, while
in all royal colonies from Maryland to South Carolina
the political victories of the assemblies resulted
sooner or later in weaker establishments. The fight
of the frontier for equitable taxation and representation did much to bring about separation of state
and church in Virginia.

We need not exaggerate the progress of religious
liberty in colonial America to establish its importance
for the growth of liberty. It can be no hardship for
modern patriots to acknowledge that the colonies
went into the Revolution with a hodgepodge of religious legislation still on the books, for the swiftness
with which the relics of privilege and discrimination
were abandoned in state after state between 1776
and 1790 is evidence that the spirit of the people had
outrun the statutes. Pennsylvania demanded belief in

God yet put no man to the test; Massachusetts taxed for support of the church yet permitted Anglicans to direct their payments to their own churches and all-out Quakers and Baptists to escape this tax completely; Rhode Island passed a law limiting political participation to Protestant Christians yet passed other laws admitting specific Jews and Catholics to citizenship; New York had an establishment in the four southern counties, yet the establishment was nameless; and Virginia swung from the most complete establishment in 1765 to freedom of religion in 1776 and full separation in 1785. In this area, too, the Revolution was over almost before it had begun.

I V

Of all the churches and sects that gained a hold in the American colonies, five or six proved popular and steadfast enough to work visible effects upon the spirit and institutions of the rising democracy. The contributions of the most prominent churches should be briefly noted.

The Society of Friends was a force to be reckoned with in the social and political life of almost every colony. From the founding of their sect the Quakers of old England had looked to the west for a refuge from persecution. Although the hopes of many leaders for a general triumph of Quaker principles in the colonies came to nothing, the ideas and methods of this most persecuted of Christian faiths helped prepare the ground for liberty.

The doctrines of the Quakers were democratic to the core, emphasizing brotherly love, mutual aid and comfort, pacifism, justice for all on equal terms, rejection of priestly authority, and religious individualism. The good Quaker, who centered his worldly thoughts upon the problem of individual conduct, would have denied that he possessed any particular theories of state and government. Yet since democracy is simply the presence of a certain number of democrats, and since the good democrat believes in principles that Quakers put first in their catalogue of virtues, it is plain that the teachings of this sect gave substance to the growing belief in the blessings of political liberty.

In practice, colonial Quakers aided the cause of liberty in several ways: their meetings were an example of democracy in being; they gave the rising nation its only real martyrs to religious persecution and fought out of principle for liberty of conscience and abolition of establishments; they provided in Pennsylvania, thanks to the rare nobility of William Penn, a "free colony for all mankind," one of the few areas in the colonies unstained by persecution; they took the lead, thanks to the even rarer nobility of John Woolman, in the movement against slavery; and they had easily the best colonial record in dealings with the Indians. The colonies in which they shared or held the reins of political power—Rhode Island, Pennsylvania, early New Jersey, early North Carolina—were the most democratic in the colonial period.

As time went by, many Quakers in prosperous, tolerant Newport and Philadelphia lost much of the old fire, surrounded as they were by slaves, wealth, and worldly power. Yet the principles remained the same, principles of liberty, justice, peace, and love; and in Virginia, the Carolinas, Massachusetts, and Maryland radical Quakerism held out strongly against oaths, tithes, military service, slavery, and social inequality. The widening social rift among "the People called Quakers" merely called attention to the democracy ingrained in their doctrine and practice.

Baptists were in the colonies almost from the beginning. Until well into the eighteenth century, however, they were few, scattered, and friendless, and were hounded severely in Massachusetts. As late as 1740, long after toleration had been secured, only about twenty Baptist congregations could be found in New England, half of these in Rhode Island. In the meantime, Baptists were flourishing in the middle colonies. Friendly Philadelphia became the center of American Baptism, and from here and the British Isles the church spread its gospel and influence into Virginia and the Carolinas. The Great Awakening had more influence on the Baptists than on any other church, and the growth of this persuasion in the years just before the Revolution was nothing short of astounding. It was a long journey from Rhode Island in 1639 to Virginia in 1776, from the twelve friends of Roger Williams to the enthusiastic horde that outnumbered the Anglicans, and one of deep significance for religious and political liberty.

The Baptists were Calvinist in theology and indeendent in church polity, differing in doctrine from New England Puritanism only in their opposition to infant baptism and to union of church and state. Their doctrine was basically illiberal and their zeal often rudely excessive. This was especially true of the Separate Baptists, who poured into Virginia and the Carolinas in the third quarter of the eighteenth century. Yet their form of church government, which emphasized the compact, equality, and congregational autonomy, nourished the growth of republican notions, as more than one royal governor acknowledged with his policy of persecution. The organization of the Baptists was more important than their theology, and their organization was as democratic as any in colonial America. Said an early historian of the Baptists, "Our religious education agrees with, and perfectly corresponds with, a government by the people."

American democracy will always be indebted to

the colonial Baptists for their single-minded devotion to complete religious liberty. Their methods were not always sensible nor their zeal free from prejudice, but their peculiar hatred for the established church, especially in Virginia, earned them lasting glory. The Baptists were the largest single group committed to complete separation of church and state. Where most other churches sought freedom within the law, the Baptists would not be satisfied until all laws on religion had been swept away completely.

The history of the Presbyterian Church in colonial America is largely a history of that multitude of eighteenth-century immigrants, the Scotch-Irish. Although Presbyterian churches or tendencies existed in the northern colonies throughout the seventeenth century, not until 1706 was the first American presbytery established, at Philadelphia under the leadership of Francis Makemie. Of the seven ministers who formed it—acting, it should be noted, on their own responsibility—six were Scotch-Irish and one a New Englander. Except for the absence of a delegate from the Dutch or German Reformed churches, which were always closely associated with Presbyterianism in doctrine and action, this proportion was representative of the relative strength of the elements making up the Presbyterian churches. The great wave of migration from Ulster to America, which began around 1710 and lasted through the Revolution, spread Scotch-Irish Presbyterianism through all the colonies, especially into the back country from Pennsylvania to the Carolinas. Puritans outside New England entered in strength into this great advancing front of Calvinism and individualism. The first synod was formed at Philadelphia in 1716.

The contributions of the Presbyterians to the rise of liberty were not quite as forceful as those of the Baptists. In both theology and organization they were a good deal more autocratic than several other prominent churches. Yet these points are certainly worth considering: their traditional emphasis on covenant and compact; their efforts to maintain a learned ministry, which led to the establishment of several colleges; the receptivity of the clergy to the Scottish philosophy of common sense and to the ideas of the Enlightenment; their activities for toleration, however much in their own interest, especially in Virginia under the devoted leadership of Samuel Davies; and the severe social disruption, the struggle between New Sides and Old Sides, that resulted from the Great Awakening. Most important of all was the unusual fact that the Scotch-Irish were generally more democratic in politics and social attitudes than in religion. In colonial Presbyterianism the stream of democracy flowed in a reverse course. Many a staunch radical in politics was a staunch conservative in religion; many a Scotch-Irish frontiersman moved from an original faith in political man to a more liberal point of view on the possibilities of universal salvation.

The German Pietist sects—Mennonites, Moravians, Schwenkfelders, Dunkers, and other groups—formed a small but vital religious element in Pennsylvania and scattered localities to the south. The common feature of these groups was their literal devotion, with the usual sectarian shadings, to the tenets of primitive Christianity: dominance of the inner spirit, private judgment, freedom of conscience, informal worship, sovereignty of the congregation (indeed of each individual who made it up), and often some form of pacifism. All these essentially democratic principles have obvious counterparts in political thought. Although the Pietists stood aloof from the push-and-pull of colonial politics, the sincerity and simplicity of their methods were yet another support to American liberty.

It is hard to make a case for Anglicanism as a force for colonial liberty, except for the left-handed manner in which its intolerance of dissent forced dissenters to redouble their efforts for toleration. An intriguing example of Anglican action that ended up producing a democratic reaction was the eighteenth-century movement—a weak movement at that—for an American bishop. The cause of political independence prospered noticeably from the outcry of opposition to this "Popish plot," and at least some of the outcry burst from Anglican throats.

Nevertheless, the development of the Anglican Church in the Southern colonies provides a useful case study of the liberalizing, or simply enfeebling, effects of the American environment on religious orthodoxy. For a variety of reasons—for example, the fact that no Bishop of London, in whose see the colonies were included, ever visited America—colonial Anglicanism was a sorry example of a hierarchical church. In Virginia the ministry grew ever more worldly and uninstructed, the parish ever more self-directing, the average adherent ever more skeptical, the discharge of devotions ever more formal, and the priestly support accorded political orthodoxy ever more strident and yet feckless. Even the devoted efforts of men like Commissaries James Blair of Virginia and Thomas Bray of Maryland and of missionaries of the Society for the Propagation of the Gospel in Foreign Parts could do little to stem the tide of laxity that seeped through American Anglicanism. Although authorities in England were inclined to agree that the ministers they sent out were "most miserably handled by their Plebeian Juntos, the Vestries," there was not much they were willing or able to do toward restoring the purity of the colonial establishment. The thoughts of able ministers in England were summarized by an Anglican missionary who complained to his superiors that he "would rather be vicar to the Bear Garden than Bishop of North Carolina."

The pattern of evolution of colonial Anglicanism was that of a hierarchical, dogmatic religion growing ever more congregational in organization and rationalist in doctrine. Although most churches remained supporters of the conservative party, and although many ministers would have no truck with the patriot cause, Anglicanism passed through the Revolution into its Episcopalian phase with little disruption or loss of continuity. This pillar of English orthodoxy was decisively Americanized in the colonial period. When Commissary Martyn of Charleston wrote his bishop in 1765, "The Principles of most of the Colonists in America are independent in Matters of Religion, as well as republican in those of Government," he could just as easily have added that this was true of some of his own ministers and most of their parishioners. Fully half the signers of the Declaration of Independence were at least nominal Anglicans.

The influence of two great and ancient religions that were later to have a massive impact on American life was hardly noticeable in the colonial period. The small numbers of Jews and slightly larger numbers of Catholics who trickled into the colonies through all this time existed so precariously and anonymously as to leave few lasting traces. Jews may take pride in the influence of the Hebraic tradition on the development of American democracy, but must acknowledge that this tradition was fed into the colonies by other hands than those of Israel. Catholics may take pride in the part played by their forefathers in the celebrated Maryland Act of Toleration (1649), but must acknowledge that this law is the most clear-cut instance in colonial history of toleration secured by religionists—Puritans and Catholics—who believed in toleration not at all. Indeed, "suffered" rather than "secured" would be the proper word in this instance, for the Act of 1649 was jammed through the Maryland Assembly on the insistence of the second Lord Baltimore, whose own motives were an undecipherable combination of principle and expediency. The honor would seem to belong to him rather than to his church. In any case, in Maryland alone in seventeenth-century America did Catholics and Protestants live side by side with any show of forbearance.

As to the eighteenth century, perhaps the less said the better. Still, it is good for modern Americans, Catholics as well as Protestants, to recall the difficulties of Catholicism in the generations before the Revolution. Of physical suffering there was little if any, for the policy of almost every colony was much simpler than that: exclusion. In this policy the English authorities concurred thoroughly. After 1679 a standard instruction to the governor of each royal colony ran:

You are to permit a liberty of conscience to all persons EXCEPT PAPISTS, so they be contented with a quiet and peaceable enjoyment of the same, not giving offense or scandal to the government.

The Catholic occupied much the same position in colonial America that the Communist does today. Though few colonists had ever seen or could have recognized a real live Catholic, they knew everything about "the Papists" and shared a morbid interest in their doctrine and practice. They were also quick to brand people Papists who were not Papists at all. The press found Catholicism excellent copy, especially if the "facts" were bloody or erotic, and especially in times of war with Catholic countries. Certainly the Catholic was feared and despised with the same unthinking passion as is the Communist today, and he was therefore the acid test of the good intentions of the new Republic. The speed with which disqualifications were erased from state laws and constitutions was, considering the heritage of hate and fear, a stunning triumph of common sense and democracy. On the eve of the Revolution mass was celebrated publicly only in easygoing Pennsylvania. On the morrow it was celebrated in every state.

V

I turn now to the two most interesting contributions of colonial religion to American liberty: one the legacy of an entire way of life, Puritanism; the other the result of the first broadly popular movement in America, the Great Awakening.

The starting point for any discussion of Puritanism and American democracy must be the unvarnished comments of the two great men of Massachusetts Bay. Said John Winthrop the magistrate: "A Democratie is, among most civill nations, accounted the meanest & worst of all formes of Governm^t . . . & Historyes doe recorde, that it hath been allwayes of least continuance & fullest of troubles." Said John Cotton the minister: "Democracy, I do not conceyve that ever God did ordeyne as a fitt government eyther for church or commonwealth. If the people be governors, who shall be governed?" Building their case on these straightforward expressions of Puritan political thought and on the historical fact of oligarchy in Massachusetts, some historians have insisted, to the distress of proud New England, that American democracy has drawn nothing from Puritanism, rather that certain nasty elements of authoritarianism in American culture may be traced directly to the Puritan strain.

These arguments are hard to meet, especially since they carry the extra weight of partial validity, but they fail to make a valid distinction between Puritans and Puritanism, between the magnificent autocrats of Boston and Salem and their inherently revolutionary way of life and thought. Whatever of good or evil we owe Winthrop and Cotton, we owe their system some of the toughest elements of our constitutional democracy. The cause of liberty and self-government in colonial America was nourished by several Puritan principles.

First, the Puritan concept of the covenant helped swell the triumph of the social contract, the dominant notion of eighteenth-century popularism. The first Puritans were obsessed with the covenant or contract, relying on this handy instrument to explain almost every relation of man to man and man to God. Of the seven or eight covenants recognized in orthodox Puritanism, the church covenant was the particular forerunner of the eighteenth-century contract. The Puritan theory of the origin of the church in the consent of the believers led directly to the popular theory of the origin of government in the consent of the governed. The doctrines of popular government held in many a Massachusetts village were largely a secularized Congregationalism. It was hardly accidental that New England ministers gave the first and most cordial reception to the arguments of John Locke and his friends and broadcast from their pulpits the new gospel of government by consent.

The Puritans were confirmed believers in higher law, going most men one better in being able to point to it in writing. The ancient Christian idea of a universal moral order appealed strongly to Calvin, even more strongly to his disciples called Puritans. It was their conviction—and here they broke sharply with the mother church in England—that the Scriptures offered correct answers to all problems of individual conduct, church government, and social and political organization. Although the Puritan determination to adhere rigidly to Hebraic mandates gave way under the stresses of human nature and the American environment, the belief in higher law—law that could be appealed to against the arbitrariness of rulers—carried over irresistibly into the developing American creed. The law of nature, like the social contract, got a warm reception among descendants of Puritans. And the traditional American insistence on a written constitution owes something to the insistence of the Puritan that higher law could be written law.

Another contribution of Puritanism to liberty was the substance it gave to the doctrine of individualism. It is strange to think of Puritanism, with its concepts of human depravity, predestination, and political authoritarianism, as a source of eighteenth-century individualism. Yet under this cruel exterior lurked notions of a liberating character, and these were to emerge in good season as a rich harvest for American democracy. Even the most rigidly orthodox Puritans betrayed suspicions that man was somehow responsible, competent, and potentially decent; that his own interpretation of Scripture, not a priest's third-hand account of revealed dogma, ought to control his actions; that salvation was the result of an inner experience, not of conformity to modes of worship; and that the way to eternity was open to all men without regard to political, economic, or social standing. Most important, Roscoe Pound has written, "Puritanism put individual judgment and individual conscience in the first place where the traditional modes of thought had put authority and the reason and judgment of the prince." In challenging the claims of hierarchy the Puritans had to stress the competence of the individual, and in so doing they opened the door to religious and political equality. The uncompromising insistence of eighteenth-century liberal preachers like Jonathan Mayhew on the "right of private judgment" was the democratic fruit of these seeds of orthodox Puritanism.

Economic individualism—a conspicuous feature of American democracy—also owes a healthy debt to Puritanism. The Puritans were anything but laissez-faire capitalists. Government regulation of the economy was an accepted part of their scheme of things. But by insisting that a godly life was both a sign of salvation and a path to prosperity, by sanctifying the virtues of industry, frugality, and self-reliance, they helped create a state of mind and morality that would make possible the rise of American capitalism. American democracy has been, in the best and truest sense of the terms, middle-class, bourgeois, free-enterprise democracy, and Puritanism did as much as any other "way of life" to give our democracy this special flavor. Puritanism was not free enterprise, but some of the best Puritans were conscious free-enterprisers, and successful ones, too.

Next, a key source of the American belief in the dependence of liberty on an educated citizenry was the Puritan emphasis on general education. Some early American radicals, most prominently Roger Williams, simply ignored the problem of education; others were hostile to the founding of schools and colleges. It was the much-maligned Puritan of Massachusetts and Connecticut—the man who insisted on a learned ministry, enlightened saints, and common men able to read the Bible and write their wills—who first showed faith in the efficacy of education. The instruments of education erected by the early New England Puritans in the face of overwhelming odds were not designed to further liberty as we understand it. Yet these instruments and the philosophy that sustained them were to prove readily convertible to the broader, more humane uses of later generations. Though few if any realized it at the time, the founding of Harvard College opened up at least one path to American liberty, as John Wise and Jonathan Mayhew were to prove to the dismay of latter-day orthodox Puritans. Harvard has been troubling the orthodox since time out of mind.

Finally, it must never be forgotten, especially in an age of upheaval and disillusionment, that American democracy rests squarely on the assumption of a pious, honest, self-disciplined, moral people. For all its faults and falterings, for all the distance it has yet to travel, American democracy has been and remains a highly moral adventure. Whatever doubts may exist about the sources of this democracy, there can be none about the chief source of the morality that gives it life and substance. From Puritanism, from the way of life that exalted individual responsibility, came those homely rules of everyday conduct—or, if we must, those rationalizations of worldly success—that have molded the American mind into its unique shape. Puritanism was the goad to the American conscience that insisted on communal responsibility before individual freedom, constitutionalism before democracy, order before liberty. If democracy has flourished in these states as strongly as anywhere in the world, it is because we are drawing still upon the moral vigor of Puritanism.

This was the legacy of Puritanism, especially of Congregational Puritanism, to American democracy: the contract and all its corollaries; the higher law as something more than a "brooding omnipresence in the sky"; the concept of the competent and responsible individual; certain ingredients of economic individualism; the insistence on a citizenry educated to understand its rights and duties; and the middle-class virtues, that high plateau of moral stability on which, so Americans believe, successful democracy must always build. When we recall that the Presbyterian, Baptist, Reformed, and even early Anglican churches in the colonies were likewise Calvinistic, we must come to the conclusion that early American Puritanism did much to give our liberty its special flavor.

VI

In the second quarter of the eighteenth century a surge of revivalistic emotion swept through the colonies. The Great Awakening, the American phase of a widespread reaction against formalism and indifference, converted tens of thousands to personal religion and left telling marks on colonial society. The spontaneity of this movement is evident in the fact that no one place could claim to be its origin, no one man its originator, no one church its chief beneficiary. The revival was aimed at re-establishing piety in all religions rather than reforming doctrine in any one.

The leading lights of the revival were Theodore Frelinghuysen of New Jersey, a Dutch Reformed minister who hit his stride about 1725; William Tennent and his four sons, Presbyterians who awakened the middle colonies in the 1730's; Jonathan Edwards, whose severe but evangelical preaching began to take effect at Northampton, Massachusetts, in 1734; and a swarm of Baptists and Presbyterians, most notably Samuel Davies, who spread the new fervor through the Southern colonies in the 1740's and later. The man whose preaching bound these diverse movements together, whose American career shows how cleanly the Awakening cut across denominational lines, was the English revivalist, George Whitefield. His glory-shouting tours through the colonies, the first beginning in Philadelphia in 1739, the last ending with his death in Newburyport in 1770, were marked by the most dramatic, effective, and well-attended preaching of the Great Awakening. He was for a generation the best-known man in colonial America. Beside him our modern revivalists pale into genteel insignificance.

The effects of the Great Awakening, especially the ways in which it hastened or delayed the day of democracy, are my concern in these few pages. As in all popular movements of this sweep, the results were mixed and the record controversial. Certainly such social by-products as the upsurge of intolerance in Connecticut and Massachusetts, the crude emotionalism of the extremist sects, and the bad feeling generated for personal reasons in dozens of communities did not benefit the fragile spirit of mutual respect upon which liberty depends. Yet for all its excesses, which revolted such religious liberals as Jonathan Mayhew and Charles Chauncy, the Great Awakening was a tremendous spur to the coming of American democracy. Here in brief were its principal democratizing effects:

The revival of piety accelerated the trend toward multiplication of religions. "If religion had been broken into segments by the Protestant revolt of the sixteenth century," Max Savelle writes, "it was atomized now by the Great Awakening of the eighteenth." All those liberating social forces which derived from the splintering of the sects were given added impetus by the schisms created in Congregationalism and Presbyterianism, by the founding of new and short-lived churches on the frontier, and by the breaking of ground for the coming of Methodism.

The increase in number of dissenting churches and the upsurge of fervor in men and women of all denominations gave new strength to the campaign for separation of church and state. Certainly disestablishment and religious liberty would not have come so swiftly in Virginia had not the Great Awakening helped create a social situation in which any other course of action would have been impractical and disruptive. The Declaration of Rights of 1776 and the Act for Establishing Religious Freedom of 1785 were made possible by changes in the religious pattern of Virginia in the 1750's and 1760's.

Equality rather than liberty or fraternity was the chief beneficiary of the Great Awakening. The revival spirit placed emphasis on the importance of the regenerated individual, without regard to his social standing, national background, calling, or religion. The rise of personalized religion among the poor folk of the colonies gave a lift to those doctrines of individual worth and social equality which were to lead the new nation to Jacksonian Democracy. By insisting that Heaven, the greatest prize of all, was open to all men on equal terms, the preachers of the Awakening aroused leveling sentiments among tens of thousands of common men.

A natural result of these new feelings of individualism and equality was the further democratizing of organization and methods in the churches. More democracy in the church led in turn to more democracy in the community, and so the great historic interaction of religion and politics continued to work to liberate man from the tyranny of the past.

If the Great Awakening led many people to distrust learning and intelligence and to insist that their ministers be no better men than they, it led other men, especially Presbyterians, to a more lively concern for education—an example of the mixed character of such broadly popular movements. William Tennent's "Log College" at Neshaminy, Pennsylvania, was the most important boost to education at the time of the Great Awakening; Princeton, Brown, Rutgers, Dartmouth, Washington and Lee, and Hampden-Sydney are modern reminders of the thorough shaking-up visited upon colonial society by the Great Awakening.

Still another product of eighteenth-century revivalism was an increase in social consciousness and humanitarianism. Some historians trace the beginnings of the antislavery movement in America to the egalitarian preaching of men like Samuel Hopkins of Great Barrington, and certainly several left-wing sects emerged from this period with new and radical attitudes on Negro slavery. The Great Awakening also revived interest in Indian missions, and everywhere there was renewed concern for abnormal and unfortunate members of society.

Finally, the revival aroused latent feelings of class antagonism. It appealed primarily to the poor and despised; it revolted the well-born, well-educated, and well-to-do. As a result, it spread like wildfire among Baptists, stirred up bitter opposition among Anglicans, and split the Presbyterian, Congregational, and Reformed churches into conservative and radical factions that conformed to class lines. Especially in Virginia, where revivalism seems to have worked the most profound changes all along the line, did eager Baptists and New Side Presbyterians awaken socially and politically as well as religiously. The challenge of religious radicalism to the formalist religion of the ruling class carried with it new doubts about the claims of this class to social and political superiority. The old habits of deference were weakened severely by the Great Awakening, not only in Virginia but all over America.

By 1765 religion in the colonies had taken on a new and unmistakable look and would henceforth be recognized as "characteristically American." The chief elements of American religion were varied and contradictory: Protestantism, especially the left-wing Puritan variety; diversity of doctrine and organization, with no one church claiming anything like a clear majority; skepticism, rationalism, and bored indifference among a large fraction of all classes; and a long-range trend toward the fact and principle of religious liberty. The blending of these elements in the colonial environment produced a pattern of faith more individualistic and liberating than that of any other Christian land. By this date, too, America's religious future had been fixed. America would be a land of religious freedom, and American politics would be conducted accordingly. Yet true religious feeling was, if anything, more widely and strongly held than in many European countries where conformity and establishment remained state policy. The principles of the awakening American democracy were to be thoroughly moral, if not indeed religious, in character. The men of 1776 believed that the good state would rise on the rock of private and public morality, that morality was in the case of most men and all states the product of religion, and that the earthly mission of religion was to set men free. It was no mere pose when they justified resistance to oppression as obedience to God and an appeal to Heaven.

IV

Self-Government before Democracy:
The Pattern of Colonial Politics

———◆———

The bisection of early American history into the years before and after the Glorious Revolution, a favorite device of colonial historians, has special application to colonial government. The first period of political development, which lasted from the Jamestown settlement (1607) to the withdrawal, alteration, and restoration of the Massachusetts charter (1684-1691), was one of "alarum and excursion" in the mother country and self-determination in the colonies. The second, which began with the creation of the Board of Trade (1696) and ended with the outburst of resistance to the Stamp Act (1765), was one of fast-growing imperial concern in England and even faster-growing political maturity in America. The influence of the first period upon the second, of the century of neglect upon the century of oversight, was great if not indeed decisive. Habits of self-government were implanted in New England and Virginia that no new policy of empire, no matter how autocratic in conception and efficient in execution, could ever have rooted out.

Except for short terms, in isolated localities, and among small groups of pioneers, there was little political democracy in the colonial period. Generations of well-meaning historians and patriots have done the colonists no service by insisting that they and their institutions were democratic. There was a good deal of practical content injected into the ancient phrase "liberty of the subject"; there were unusual opportunities for self-government at all levels; and there was thinking and talking about democracy that outran actual performance. Yet for the most part government in the colonies was simply a less corrupt and oppressive, more popular and easygoing version of government at home, and thus was characterized by limited suffrage, aristocratic leadership, and both deference and indifference among the mass of men. The governments of the continental colonies were a stage in the development of American democracy rather than democracy itself. The thoughts of good colonists were thoughts of liberty and self-government rather than of equality and mass participation. The course of political freedom was halting, full of starts and stops and discouraging retreats, yet over the generations it went slowly and painfully upward to ultimate triumph.

I

The pattern of government in each colony was determined by its "constitution," leading elements of which were the original charter, grant, or patent and its renewals, commissions, and instructions to the governor, orders-in-council and other directions from the mother country, codes of laws, and local custom and practice. The charter, grant, or patent was the basic document; there were three kinds of charter and thus three types of colony in early America:

The royal colony was, from a constitutional point of view, a political entity in which the Crown was immediately supreme and sovereign. In theory, all officials and institutions existed at the pleasure of the King; in practice, the colonists shared heavily in determining their political destinies, especially through the assembly and institutions of local government.

The royal colony was easily the most satisfactory type in terms of English interests. Had the early imperialists had their way, royal government would have been installed without delay throughout the empire. Even though it was not, the trend toward centralization of power in the Crown went on apace, and by the middle of the eighteenth century eight of thirteen colonies were royal in constitution: Virginia, New York, New Hampshire, Massachusetts, New Jersey, North Carolina, South Carolina, and Georgia.

The proprietary was a colony in which political power and ownership of the land were placed in the hands of one or more private individuals. The model of such proprietaries as Maryland and the Carolinas was the county palatine of Durham, a feudal principality in which the Bishop of Durham, for reasons of state, had been granted the powers of a virtually absolute king. Because of weaknesses inherent in its constitutional structure, which took little time coming to the surface in the wilderness, the proprietary was pretty much a failure in colonial America. Some proprietorships were converted into royal colonies; others made such heavy concessions to imperial demands from above and popular urges from below as to be scarcely distinguishable from royal colonies. Although nine colonies were originally constituted as proprietorships under royal favor, only three—Pennsylvania, Delaware, and Maryland—were in existence in 1765.

Connecticut and Rhode Island, both founded without authority from the Crown, were granted royal charters of incorporation at the time of the Restoration. Despite repeated threats of judicial or legislative revocation, they clung to their corporate charters and unique status of independence throughout the eighteenth century. In these two colonies the pattern of self-government was most firmly established. Although the Crown retained considerable authority over their military, diplomatic, and commercial affairs, the extent of supervision was spotty and discontinuous. An especially sour Tory, John Mein of Boston, was not too far from the truth when he wrote of Connecticut and Rhode Island: "The people in those Colonies chuse their Governors, Judges, Assemblymen, Counsellors, and all the rest of their Officers; and the King and Parliament have as much influence there as in the wilds of Tartary." In the commonwealth period (1630-1684) Massachusetts was an extraordinary type of corporate colony—extraordinary alike in origin, form, and pretensions to independence. Although the charter of 1691 established Massachusetts as a royal colony, the corporate features were never entirely eradicated.

The governor—in the royal colonies a viceroy appointed by the King, in the proprietaries an agent selected by the proprietors, in Connecticut and Rhode Island a local gentleman chosen by the assembly—was the key official in each of the colonies. In the royal and proprietary colonies he was the focus of internal politics and external relations. As representative of the sponsoring agency in England, especially of the Crown, he exercised most of the ancient executive prerogatives: command of the forces; the summoning, proroguing, and dissolution of the assembly; an absolute veto over legislation; appointment to subordinate offices; leadership of the church wherever established; the royal prerogative of mercy; oversight, at least by instruction, in financial affairs; and often, with the council, the responsibility of serving as the colony's court of last resort. In short, he was the symbol and fact of imperial authority—a dignified chief of state, a powerful political and military official, a direct participant in legislative and judicial affairs, and the linchpin of empire.

Over against the governor, representative of England and monarchy, was set the assembly, representative of colony and people. The political and constitutional history of colonial America appears often to have been nothing so much as a huge, ill-tempered tug-of-war between governors and assemblies, and it was the latter that grew steadily more robust in the struggle for power. Some assemblies were established under royal, proprietary, or trading-company favor; others were spontaneous creations of the men on the spot. Grounded firmly in representative and electoral systems that were the direct ancestors of present American practice, converted sooner or later by circumstance into a bicameral structure (everywhere except Pennsylvania), persuaded through experience that they could wield all the traditional powers and privileges of a legislature, the assemblies were the most important instruments of popular government in colonial America. The growth of such techniques of representation as residence requirements, constituency payments, annual elections, instructions, voting by ballot, and bans on place-holding by assemblymen is evidence that the assemblies were far more advanced toward the idea of a popular legislature than was the House of Commons.

In each colony there was also a conciliar body, generally made up of twelve gentlemen of property and prestige, which exercised important functions of an executive, legislative, and judicial character. The council acted for the governor as advisory cabinet, with the assembly as upper house of a bicameral legislature, and again with the governor as highest provincial court of appeals in civil cases (and in Virginia in criminal cases as well). It was often as powerful an agent of royal authority as the governor. The normal method of appointment of councilors was by the Crown, on recommendation of the governor. The principal instance of deviation from this scheme was to be found in Massachusetts. The charter of 1691, which could not ignore the years of republican independence, provided for a council of twenty-eight to be chosen annually by the general court subject to the veto of the governor.

In its origins and early development the judicial system of colonial America paid scant attention to English precedents. In the seventeenth century the differences between the courts of one colony and the next were so pronounced that it is impossible to make any general statement about them. What existed in most colonies was a practical system of law and courts in which there was much emphasis on the colonists' own rude notions of justice and little on uniform practice or a trained bench and bar. In Massachusetts lawyers were forbidden to practice, and in all colonies the prejudice against them was surprisingly strong. In part this could be traced to English antecedents; the Fundamental Constitutions of Carolina labeled it "a base and vile thing to plead for money or reward." In part it was the natural reaction of a frontier society to a profession identified with the complexities of civilization.

In the eighteenth century, chiefly at the behest of the Crown and under the pressures of a maturing society, the trend was everywhere toward uniformity in organization and improvement in professional standards. By 1765 the judicial system in most colonies was regularized and independent, and the chief agents of the system, the lawyers, were climbing into the political saddle. The remarkably fair trial of Captain John Preston and his men for the Boston Massacre and the overwhelming resistance of the judiciary to general writs of assistance are proof of the vitality of the court system inherited by the Revolutionary generation.

II

No account of government in colonial America would be complete without some mention of the complexity of officials active in England and the colonies as agents of the Crown's belated attempt to prosecute a consistent imperial policy. The word "complexity" is used advisedly, for in the eighteenth century there were so many officials and committees engaged in overseeing the colonies that it is almost impossible to fix with exactness their powers, functions, and relations to one another. Several features of imperial administration, however, are beyond dispute. Control of the colonies was exercised in the name of the King and thus as an extraordinary assertion of the royal prerogative, which by this time had lost most of its meaning in the mother country. Parliament, which was preoccupied with weightier affairs, was quite unsure of its right to legislate in support or restraint of this last significant manifestation of the prerogative. Neither Crown nor Parliament created much in the way of special machinery for colonial affairs, and for the most part regular executive agencies expanded their activities to include the colonies. Final authority over the colonies resided in the Privy Council, but the actual task of supervision was carried on by committees of the Council, regular agencies, and one specially constituted board. The most important of these varied instruments were:

The Board of Trade, or "Lords Commissioners of Trade and Plantations," was a staff and advisory agency independent of the Privy Council. The Board was charged with drafting instructions for the governors, hearing colonial complaints, suggesting appointments, collecting information for purposes of more effective oversight and direction, and reviewing colonial laws. Although the Board was inferior in legal status and had no sanctions at its command, it wielded much influence through its correspondence with governors and through reports and recommendations to the Crown. Rarely did the Privy Council disregard its advisory verdict on the wisdom or legality of colonial legislation.

The Committee of the Privy Council, often known as "the Lords of the Committee of Council for hearing appeals and complaints from the plantations," was an agency whose functions are clear in its title. This committee provided, for those colonists able and willing to make use of its machinery, a reasonably impartial and efficient high court of appeals. Its chief purpose was not to do justice or develop an imperial common law, but to protect prerogative and mercantilism against colonial interference.

The Treasury Board dealt with the larger problems of colonial finance, especially in time of war, and exercised important discretion in settling American claims for money.

The Commissioners of the Customs, an agency of the Treasury, took the lead in enforcing the Navigation Acts and collected the duties levied under them. The commissioners drafted special instructions to the governors in matters of trade and revenue and tendered advice to other branches of the government concerning commercial policy.

The Admiralty directed the navy's commercial and martial operations in American waters.

The War Office, which first came into prominence in the French and Indian War, was the agency for organizing and equipping the British armies in America.

Last in order, but in many ways first in importance, was the Secretary of State for the Southern Department, the chief official for colonial affairs in the developing cabinet system. The first concern of the

Secretary of State was war and diplomacy with France and Spain; his conduct of office thus bore directly upon problems of security for the colonies. The makings of a unified system of colonial control were present in this office, but for several reasons— the lack of interest in colonial affairs of most incumbents, the preoccupation of the Secretary with the over-all pattern of war and diplomacy, and the rapid turnover in personnel—these potentialities were never realized.

The result of this conjunction of too much organization for detail and too little concern for unity— especially when intensified by distance, slowness of communication, inferiority of personnel, corruption, bribery, and colonial obstinacy—was a large measure of self-government for the colonies. Each of the chief weapons of imperial control—the viceregal authority of the governor, appeals to the Privy Council, and royal disallowance of colonial legislation—proved defective or inadequate in action. The governor was one thing in the instructions of the Board of Trade, quite another in Williamsburg, Boston, or New York. The system of appeals to the Privy Council was workable enough, but was confined to cases in which a sizable sum was at stake. In the entire colonial period less than two hundred cases from the American colonies were prosecuted before the Council. Whatever it was to become in later years, it was not in the eighteenth century a supreme court of empire. The extent of imperial control exercised through the technique of royal disallowance may be judged from the figures: From 1691 to the end of the colonial period roughly 8,500 laws were submitted for approval. Of these some 470, or 5.5 per cent, were disallowed. The practice of submission and examination was loose and was particularly hampered by the fact of distance. Considerable success was achieved by English authorities in blocking laws that encroached on the prerogative, affected England's commercial interests, interfered with the established church, tampered with the currency, and altered the laws of inheritance; yet for the most part the threat of royal disallowance had surprisingly little effect on the course of colonial self-government.

All sorts of officials were active in the colonies as instruments of royal supervision and control. Of these the most important in each colony were the royal governor, his council, and such executive officials as the secretary and attorney general. In addition, strewn through all the colonies, even in self-contained Rhode Island and Connecticut, was an ever-growing band of emissaries and executors for the agencies at home: naval officers, customs officials, military and naval commanders, deputy postmasters, and judges of vice-admiralty. "He has erected a multitude of New Offices," Jefferson complained in the Declaration of Independence, "and sent hither swarms of Officers to harass our people, and eat out their substance."

One of the interesting developments of the colonial period was the establishment by the colonies of permanent representatives at the seat of empire—a development that was encouraged by the Board of Trade. The duties of the colonial agent, who was generally an American resident in England, were determined largely by circumstance: to represent the interests of the colony before the agencies of imperial control; to gather and transmit information in both directions; to see to the colony's commercial, financial, and judicial interests; and generally to further its fortunes in all possible ways, even (as in the famous instances of Dummer and Franklin) to the extent of writing pamphlets to influence English opinion. As the split between governor and assembly widened in the eighteenth century, it became common practice for each of these political branches to maintain its own agent. By the time of the Revolution eight assemblies had agents in London, most of whom were named Benjamin Franklin.

Such was the scheme of government at the center and extremities of empire—at the center a hodge-podge of administration with standards of solicitude and performance that varied radically from one agency to another and from one period to the next, at the extremities a swarm of officials dedicated either to Crown or to colony, rarely to both. The push and pull of these opposing forces is the substance of American political and constitutional history in the eighteenth century.

III

If the pattern of colonial politics was marked by a growing measure of self-government and home rule, then the question arises: Who were the "selves" who did the governing? Who ruled at home? An answer can be found by considering three related problems: the nature of the suffrage in the various colonies; the extent to which the suffrage was actually exercised; the intensity of popular interest and participation in affairs of town and colony.

The history of the colonial suffrage, like the history of almost all early American institutions, was one of primitive diversity in the seventeenth century and maturing uniformity in the eighteenth. A wide variety of practice prevailed before 1690, ranging from the narrow limitation of church membership in Massachusetts to something quite close to white manhood suffrage during the first years in Virginia, Rhode Island, West Jersey, and several other localities. As the settlements developed into more stable societies, demands arose for a broader suffrage in the autocratic colonies and a narrower one in the popular. By the turn of the century, some sort of property qualification for voting had been established in every colony, and this feature of American politics continued in force until well after the winning of independence. In part the requirement of property-holding was fostered by English authorities, who had begun to insist in charters and instructions that

You shall take care that the members of the assembly be elected only by *ffreeholders*, as being more agreeable to the custome of England, to which you are as nigh as conveniently you can to conforme yourselfe.

In part it could be traced to the fact that the colonists, too, were Englishmen and therefore felt, consciously or unconsciously, the urge to conform to ancient ways. It was inevitable that men of their blood and traditions should be impelled by the rise of a propertied class to restrict the suffrage to those who were in it.

The details of these property requirements furnish yet another instance of English practice adapted to American conditions. In most colonies the basic qualification was the famous "forty-shilling freehold." Seven of them—New Hampshire, Rhode Island, New York, New Jersey, Virginia, North Carolina, and Georgia—made the possession of land an absolute requirement; the others recognized property other than real estate. Everywhere a "stake-in-society" was the door to political enfranchisement, and almost everywhere additional restrictions kept women, youths, Catholics, Jews, infidels, Negroes, Indians, mulattoes, indentured servants, and other "inferior" persons from the polls. A few, but only a very few, voices were lifted in protest against limited suffrage. Perhaps the clearest of these spoke through an advertisement in a Philadelphia newspaper in 1737:

A PECUNIARY Gratification is offered to any of the learned or unlearned, who shall *Mathematically* prove, that a Man's having a Property in a Tract of Land, more or less, is

thereby entitled to any Advantage, *in point of understanding*, over another Fellow, who has no other Estate, than
"THE AIR ... *to breathe in*, THE EARTH ... *to walk upon*, and ALL THE RIVERS OF THE WORLD ... *to drink of*."

Accurate figures of the voting potential in each colony are not easy to establish. The best estimate would be that something like one out of every four white males was eligible to vote for representatives in the assembly, perhaps one out of three for elective officers in towns and in boroughs with open charters of incorporation. There were many deviations, both upward and downward, from these averages, depending, for example, upon the local price and availability of land, proximity to the frontier, and the origins and attitudes of the inhabitants. It must be emphasized that these figures are estimates only, for reliable statistics are just not to be found.

If these figures are discouraging to those who think of the colonies as a Paradise Lost of American democracy, even more discouraging are estimates of exercise of the suffrage. Again the pattern is one of extreme variation from one time and locality to the next, but in general there existed what appears at first glance to have been an attitude of astounding apathy toward campaigns and elections. Not only was but one in four white males eligible to vote; in many places but one in four of those eligible even bothered to vote. Records of the late eighteenth century show that in several supposedly hotly contested elections in Massachusetts an average of one qualified voter in five took the trouble to vote. The figures are better, but not too much better, in Virginia and the middle colonies. Apathy toward elections was a widespread feature of colonial politics, and there were no campaigns to "get out the vote."

The third point of inquiry, the intensity of popular interest and participation in affairs of town and colony, has already been largely answered. What was true of voting was doubly true of office-holding: Restrictions were many and aspirants few. In an age when breadwinning consumed all a man's time and energy, when travel was difficult and political parties nonexistent, when government was severely limited in scope and touched many men not at all, and when the pace of life went slowly, political indifference— to elections, to office-holding, and to issues—was well-nigh inevitable. Despite eloquent references to "an aroused people" in certain memorable debates in the assemblies, politics in colonial America was the province of those with particular interests to defend or with a natural flair for public action. The number of such persons was never and nowhere very large. The political apathy of the colonial press, punctured only occasionally before 1765 by a thorough airing of some local squabble, is proof of the slow pace of political life. "Publick Lethargy" was under constant attack by colonial penmen.

This does not mean that the declarations and decisions of the attentive few or the experiences and instincts of the indifferent many were any the less important to the progress of American liberty. The few in their assemblies, town meetings, and polls held the democratic future in trust and acted out on a small stage the great drama of constitutional government that was in time to call millions into the supporting cast. The many, too, had their notion of liberty and self-government: to be left alone to pursue their own destinies. When government became important or oppressive enough, they found ways other than politics to express their wishes and to influence action. Sullen resistance, riots, and "going out west" are not generally recommended as effective techniques of political freedom, but in colonial times they served a very real purpose.

These are the facts of political participation in the American colonies: Only a fraction could participate and even a lesser fraction did; the colonies were still well ahead of practice in almost all other countries; and many men never cared one way or the other about political power. Nor should it be forgotten that in a society so amazingly fluid for the age, a society where people could "move on" and where land was cheap and plentiful, the privilege of the suffrage was something that almost any white man could win. The records prove that everywhere, even in aristocratic New York and South Carolina, men of mean birth and menial occupation could aspire to political power and prominence. And that a man in eighteenth-century Virginia or New England had neither opportunity nor desire to vote or hold office did not mean that he considered himself a slave. In an age when politics was one of the least of man's worries, the poll lists were one of the lesser criteria of the progress of liberty.

I V

Seeds of contention between governor and assembly were sown with profusion in the constitutions of the eleven royal or proprietary colonies. The inherent contradiction between the interests and attitudes of the mother country and those of the distant colonies was especially apparent in this instance. On one hand stood the royal or proprietary governor—in four cases out of five an Englishman, in the fifth a loyal colonial, in any case an agent of the prerogative with a commission and instructions that made him an autocrat not beholden to colonial direction. On the other stood the provincial assembly—the articulate organ of a breed of men who were more English than the English in their obstinacy, pride, and hypersensitivity in matters of self-government. From the outset the system gaped at the middle, and the final triumph of the assembly was almost foreordained. Although the governor occupied a position of over-whelming constitutional superiority, it was undercut repeatedly by circumstances in colony and empire.

The governors got far more verbal than practical support from the authorities at home. The remote-ness of colonial capitals and the lack of either an imperial policy or the will to execute it created a situation in which the governor was left pretty much on his own. It was he, not the Board of Trade, who had to live with the colonists; it was his estimate of the expedient, not the Board's demand of the im-possible, that controlled decisions taken on the spot. The governor was too often left defenseless against what Governor Clinton of New York labeled the as-sembly's "continued Grasping at Power."

The colonists fell naturally into an opinion of their governors best summed up in Franklin's remark about "men of vicious characters and broken fortunes, sent by a Minister to get them out of the way." We know today that this was rarely the case, that the gover-nors were neither better nor worse than the officials who carried on the public business of England. There were men as bad as Cornbury and Fletcher, but there were also men as good as Dinwiddie, the Wentworths, Spotswood, Hunter, Pownall, Burnet, Shirley, Glen, and Dobbs. No matter who the governors were, how-ever, most colonists agreed with the New York As-sembly of 1749 that they were

generally entire Strangers to the People they are sent to govern . . . their Interest is entirely distinct . . . they seldom regard the Welfare of the People, otherwise than as they can make it subservient to their own particular Interest.

In this instance the myth was more telling than the fact, and the myth was one of "men of broken fortunes, dissolute and ignorant, too vile to be em-ployed near home," a calumny that the English press

printed and the colonial press reprinted with glee
Recognition of the alien purposes of the royal governors and misrepresentation of their personal traits did
much to strengthen the morale and ambitions of the
colonial assemblies, not that they needed it.

Colonial legislators were persistent, clever, and
vigilant, and over the years they advanced a surprisingly coherent policy in constitutional matters. The
struggle for power was not always so bitter and decisive as some history books would have it, for several
colonies enjoyed extended periods of political quies-
cence and good will. Yet the trend of power moved
almost always toward the assembly, which used this
power to fight its way ever higher in the name of
"the people" and "our ancient and undoubted rights
and priviledges as Englishmen."

The lack of real toughness in the imperialists in
England permitted the colonists to exploit to the
limit the fatal defect of the colonial constitutions:
the location of the power of the purse in colonial
hands, a defect compounded by the failure of the
Crown to provide a permanent civil list in any of the
colonies. No one was more aware than the governor
himself that, in Governor Bernard's words, "the Want
of a certain and adequate civil List to each Colony"
was "the Root of the American Disorders." Far too
many officials, institutions, and necessities of empire
were left dependent upon the willingness of the assemblies to tax friends and neighbors and thus upon
the natural desire to fix conditions upon any and all
grants.

Occasionally in spectacular political warfare accom-
panied by newspaper attacks on the governors, but
more often through unpublicized day-to-day en-
croachments, the assemblies grasped for privileges
and powers like those of the House of Commons.
Several of Parliament's hard-earned privileges—con-

trol over procedure, freedom of debate, determination of disputed elections—were secured by the assemblies. Others—the "Speaker's Petition," control over sessions, regulation of elections, creation of new electoral districts—were not, and over these the struggle raged in almost every colony. The Crown defended with tenacity the governor's power to prorogue and dissolve the assembly and the final weapons of gubernatorial veto and royal disallowance. Yet the area of assembly freedom grew ever wider, especially as it came home to more and more colonists that the fight for parliamentary privilege was at bottom a fight for the liberty of the subject.

The assemblies also used the purse to pry their way into executive affairs. For example, by designating a specific person to receive the salary of an office they usurped the power of appointment; by naming their own committees and even their own treasurer to verify expenditures they encroached substantially on the governor's command of the militia and control over military stores; and by the famous expedient of tampering with the governor's salary they brought more than one recalcitrant to heel in such matters as personnel and jurisdiction of colonial courts. The governors of Georgia and Virginia were the only viceroys whose salaries were not dependent on the pleasure of the assembly or, as in the case of the North Carolina quit rents, on an unsatisfactory substitute arrangement. Especially acrimonious battles were fought in New York and Massachusetts over the assembly's calculated practice of annual grants to the governor—with the assembly emerging victorious. The provision in the Constitution of 1787 forbidding the raising or lowering of the President's compensation attests the respect in which eighteenth-century Americans held this technique.

By 1765 the assembly was dominant in almost every colony in continental America. The royal power of disallowance was still strong enough to prevent a complete overriding of the governor and other imperial officials, but shrewd observers were beginning to realize that only the full power of Parliament was now equal to the centrifugal practices of the assemblies. Most discouraging to proponents of empire was the inability of English authorities to secure positive accomplishments. The record of colonial co-operation, or rather non-co-operation, in time of war must have been hard to swallow. The assemblies recorded their most spectacular gains, especially in their campaign to control the public purse, in the French and Indian War. More than one governor must have felt that he rather than the French was the enemy to be reduced to a plea for mercy.

The struggles of the colonial assemblies provide an instructive example of the way in which men distrustful of democracy in one century can, by fighting for their own privileges and opinions, open the way to democracy in the next. Indeed, "distrustful of democracy" is the very best that can be said of cliques that controlled assemblies in New Hampshire, Pennsylvania, the Carolinas, and Virginia. The records show up many colonial parliamentarians as illtempered, petty, self-seeking, tiresome little men more often than not committed to the intolerant side of questions of religious and social freedom. Yet the assemblies also counted an unusual range of strong and able men, many of whom were genuinely progressive in their opinions. The Whigs in the colonial legislatures had a limited popularism as their goal, but in driving toward it they unloosed forces that would not be halted short of total political democracy. And their arguments proved in time to be fully convertible to democratic currency.

The colonial assemblies, like the dissenting churches, were influential schools of American political thought. The system under which delegates were chosen was one as representative of "the people" as could be erected in those days of concern for Whig ideals of liberty. The proceedings of the assemblies were open to public inspection and criticism, their journals were printed and distributed, and their exchanges with the governors, especially those of a pungent nature, got thorough coverage in the colonial press. Just about all that the people of South Carolina knew of Massachusetts was that there, too, the assembly hacked away resolutely at the governor's position and powers. There can be no argument with Charles M. Andrews's conclusion: "In the development of American political ideas and social practices, the influence of the popular assembly . . . is the most potent single factor underlying our American system of government."

V

Self-sustaining institutions of local government have always been a sure sign of political freedom. The flourishing condition of such institutions in colonial times was at once a factor in the evolution of democratic principles and evidence of the progress of American liberty. It was evidence of other things as well: the English origins of the founders of the various colonies; the remarkable display of pragmatic ingenuity, or of plain horse sense, that they devoted to fitting their inherited experience to new conditions of geography and economic structure; the intense political self-reliance of the first settlers and their descendants; and the widespread distrust of arbitrary or centralized government. In general, the central governments of the colonies exercised even less control over local institutions than did the mother country over the colonies. Self-government was doubly the rule in colonial America.

The over-all pattern of local government was typ-

ically colonial, exhibiting primitive diversity in the
seventeenth century, maturing uniformity in the
eighteenth, and sharp differences always between
North and South, frontier and seaboard, city and village. In New England the incidence of local self-
direction was especially pronounced. The basic units
were the county, which in most of New England was
a judicial-military district but in Massachusetts handled problems of land titles, probate administration,
highway planning, licensing, and taxation as well, and
the town, which dealt with "prudential affairs": care
of highways, poor relief, preservation of the peace,
elementary education, land disposal and registration,
assessment and collection of taxes and tithes, and
just about any other matter of local interest, including the enforcement of "blue laws." The county's affairs were directed by justices and other officers appointed by the governor, who rarely if ever
ignored local opinion in making his selections. There
was no representative body for county affairs, nor
does there seem to have been any demand for one.

Although colonial assemblies passed many laws
dealing with the organization and powers of the
towns, these units were in fact quite independent of
central control. More important, they were self-
governing in the most obvious sense—through the
famous town meeting, the selectmen, and a host of
unpaid minor officials: constables, tithingmen, sur-
veyors, fence-viewers, field-drivers, haywards, no-
tice-givers, assessors, pound-keepers, corders of wood,
leather-sealers, overseers of the poor, "hogg constables," cutters of fish, and "cometies" for almost
every conceivable purpose, all chosen from and by
the citizenry. In 1720 an average Massachusetts town,
Ipswich, had ninety-seven regular officials.

Town government in colonial New England has
never deserved more than a fraction of the encomi-
ums heaped indiscriminately upon it, for the records

tell us that polite oligarchy and careless apathy were common in those days, too. The same names appear year after year in important offices; the same concern over nonattendance at town meeting is displayed in resolves ordering delinquents to show up or be fined. Yet the town was a species of artless democracy, however limited; it was far more popular a scheme of government than local institutions in the homeland; and it provided, for those who took part in elections, meetings, and public service, important schooling in the techniques of political freedom. The town governments of New England were, quite without hyperbole, the most memorable form of local self-government in colonial America.

Local government in the Southern colonies was aristocratic, even oligarchical in character. In neither of the two major units, county and parish, were officers elected, nor was there any sort of representative body. The county—the key unit for military, judicial, administrative, and electoral affairs—was governed by a court of eight or more justices appointed by the governor on recommendation of the justices themselves. In practice, this converted the court into a closed, self-perpetuating organ of the local gentry. The parish, which was much less important than the county and dealt with such problems as government of the local church, ferries, land boundaries, and care of the poor, was equally closed and self-perpetuating. Yet in the vital tests of self-reliance and freedom from central supervision, the counties and parishes of Virginia and South Carolina were as typically colonial as the towns of New England. The select vestries of Bristol and Stratton Major were not too different in character from the selectmen of Little Compton and Simsbury. The records give much substance to Jefferson's observations on the vestrymen:

These are usually the most discreet farmers, so distributed through their parish, that every part of it may be under the immediate eye of some one of them. They are well acquainted with the details and economy of private life, and they find sufficient inducements to execute their charge well, in their philanthropy, in the approbation of their neighbors, and the distinction which that gives them.

Local government in the middle colonies was neither as popular as in the North nor select as in the South. New York and Pennsylvania went through their own processes of evolution, which in each instance led to selection of the county as the principal unit. County government in New York was in the hands of a board of supervisors; each town in the county elected one member of this board. In Pennsylvania a law of 1724 established a somewhat different system under which three commissioners were elected from the whole county to manage fiscal, civil, and judicial affairs. These two systems were destined to spread from New York and Pennsylvania throughout the Union. They, too, were marked by a considerable degree of self-determination in the colonial period. The town meeting was carried into several areas of the middle colonies, but failed to take fast root except in the settlements on Long Island. There —in Oyster Bay, Southampton, Huntington, and other still-pleasant towns—descendants of New Englanders governed themselves in the New England way.

Two special types of local arrangement were relatively uniform in appearance and spirit through most of the colonies: government in the incorporated city, and government on the frontier. Many of the more populous localities—Boston, Baltimore, New Haven, Newport, Charleston—were governed through most or all of the colonial period under much the same forms as were their small neighbors. Others—including such important centers as New York, Albany, Philadelphia, Annapolis, Norfolk, and

Williamsburg, as well as a dozen or so lesser communities—were granted charters of incorporation. Several of these were "close" corporations, in which mayor, councilors, aldermen, and other officials were empowered to choose their own successors. The majority, however, enjoyed charters of a more popular character. In New York, for example, councilors and aldermen were elected by the freemen and freeholders of the borough. Colonial incorporations exercised almost complete control over their own affairs, and in several of them political activity reached its peak in the colonial period. The independence of local units was dramatically demonstrated in 1734 by the refusal of officials of the city of New York to obey Governor Cosby's order to attend the burning of the offensive numbers of John Peter Zenger's *Weekly Journal*.

We know very little about the politics of the wilderness. The chief sources of information are the priceless records of the very first settlements, when the frontier was everywhere and every man a frontiersman. These records tell us that a practical, primitive householders' democracy, grounded in the fact and theory of free consent, was the usual form of government in almost every English settlement except Massachusetts Bay. Later pioneers, especially the Scotch-Irish in Pennsylvania, Virginia, and the Carolinas, were not so literate and articulate as Roger Williams and John Pory, yet we learn something of their ways through occasional minutes, letters, and travelers' descriptions. The picture is one of the barest bones of government. Yet even in this state of near-anarchy there was active that peculiar combination of individualism and co-operation—"free association"—which was enforced by circumstances of the agrarian frontier. When organs of town, parish, or county government were finally set up in the settlements, they were cast in a rudely popular mold. The institutions were those of the tidewater, but the spirit and suffrage were those of the frontier.

By way of summation, these common features of local government in the colonies should be noted: the broader suffrage for local than for colony-wide elections; the multiplicity of unpaid offices and duties, a system under which a much larger percentage of citizens performed some sort of public duty than is the case today; the healthy publicity that went along with government by "friends and neighbors"; the absence of control, supervision, and tampering by governor or assembly; the limited scope of service as contrasted with modern local government; and the devotion of the average man's political attention to affairs of town rather than colony. All these are signs of a pragmatic sort of popularism, which was especially strong in the New England towns, frontier settlements, and open boroughs. Historians were later to rhapsodize about the "democracy" of these experiments, but the colonists valued them for their simplicity and utility. Whatever their worth as instruments of public service, these institutions taught the colonists one more sturdy lesson in freedom from pomp and arbitrary power.

VI

By 1765 the minds and consciences of a healthy number of Americans had been sharpened to a lively concern for political liberty. Unsophisticated and intuitive as colonial notions of liberty might seem to us today, they were held in such esteem and expressed with such fervor as to work decisive influence on the course of events. The early colonists—good Englishmen they were—had talked incessantly of their rights and privileges. As the settlements progressed toward social maturity and political self-consciousness, developments in assembly and local government gave new content to old phrases. From this experience flowed new ideas of liberty, and these ideas in turn gave rise to even more liberty. By the middle of the eighteenth century the spirit of freedom was flourishing in the colonies far more vigorously than in England. "They augur misgovernment at a distance," Burke cried, "and snuff the approach of tyranny in every tainted breeze." What Tories derided and feared as "republican notions" had swept America from leveling Vermont to aristocratic Charleston.

Most of the liberties that are generally associated with constitutional democracy are mentioned at other points in this book: suffrage, elections, assembly privileges, and equality before the law; liberty of individual conscience and separation of church and state; freedom of opportunity and social mobility; free inquiry and the right to dissent from political or religious orthodoxy. All these liberties were developing at different speeds in different colonies, most vigorously on the frontier and in the cities of the northern and middle colonies. There were people everywhere who cherished and enjoyed them, and who were ready at the snuff of a tainted breeze to defend them with philosophical and practical argument—and ultimately with their blood.

Let me concentrate here on one basic liberty. Freedom of press—the uncontrolled and uncensored exchange in print of ideas, information, arguments, and accusations—is in many ways the essential political liberty. The effective conduct of free government is dependent upon the existence of a free press; the fortunes of each seem always to rise and fall together. The establishment of a free press in eighteenth-century America was therefore a fact of great moment for the future Republic. The struggle for a free and unlicensed press was long and frustrating, but by the time of the Stamp Act the victory had been sealed. In seventeenth-century America there was no such thing as freedom of press. Indeed, in many colonies there was no press at all. The disrupting power of the printed word was well understood by those who ruled in Europe and America. Governor Berkeley of Virginia was only a trifle tougher than his fellow autocrats when he wrote to the lords commissioners in 1671:

But, I thank God, *there are no free schools* nor *printing*; and I hope we shall not have these hundred years; for *learning* has brought disobedience, and heresy, and sects into the world, and *printing* has divulged them, and libels against the best government. God keep us from both!

A standard royal command issued to governors between 1686 and 1732 was this:

Forasmuch as great inconveniences may arise by the liberty of printing in our said province, you are to provide by all necessary orders that no person keep any press for printing, nor that any book, pamphlet, or other matters whatsoever be printed without your especial leave and license first obtained.

In the few places where printing presses were permitted in the seventeenth-century settlements, they were sponsored or watched closely by the ruling authorities. Massachusetts took the lead: A press was established at Cambridge in 1638 for orthodox purposes, and thirty-odd years later Marmaduke Johnson set up, under strict licensing, another press in Boston. It was here on September 25, 1690, that *Publick Occurrences*, America's first newspaper, appeared—and was immediately suppressed.

The rise of a free press was therefore a development of the eighteenth century. The bare facts of this development indicate its extent and character: In 1715 there was one newspaper in the colonies, John Campbell's weekly *Boston News-Letter*, which carried news of England a year old, had a circulation of 250, and was "published by authority." In 1765 there were twenty-three, at least one in each colony but New Jersey and Delaware, carrying news and letters of every variety and political hue, reaching tens of thousands of subscribers and their friends, and being printed everywhere without censorship and almost everywhere without fear of governor or assembly. Several of these were already quite partisan in character, while others discharged their obligations to free discussion by publishing documents and letters on all sides of an issue, thus fulfilling the motto of Rind's *Virginia Gazette*: "Open to All Parties but influenced by None." Until 1765 the press engaged for the most part in straight reporting, with emphasis on "European Intelligence" (especially war news and speculation about such problems as the Queen of Denmark's rupture and the Queen of Spain's "inward Disorders"), ship arrivals and clearings, exchanges of pleasantries between King and Parliament, horror stories, moralizing, and essays on such subjects as "The Faithfulness of Dogs" and "Early Rising."

The decision of Parliament to tax the colonies brought the press to life. The reaction of newspapers to the Stamp Act was clamorous and unanimous. The transition from political apathy to political frenzy was especially noticeable in such newspapers as the *Georgia Gazette, Pennsylvania Journal, Connecticut Gazette, South-Carolina Gazette, New-York Gazette, New-York Mercury,* and above all the *Boston Gazette.* In 1763 some of these journals were devoting eleven in twelve columns to paid advertisements; in 1765 they were devoting eleven in twelve to letters from Britannicus Americanus, A Friend to Both Peoples, Sydney, and Mucius Scaevola.

Of equal importance in this development was the increasingly vigorous practice of political pamphleteering. The astounding success of Paine's *Common*

Sense was made possible by decades of other pamphlets that had helped transfer this habit from England to America. Much less significant politically, but no less interesting, were the fourteen magazines that were published for brief intervals during these years.

We should pay tribute to the journalists who did most to defy authority in the struggle for an uncensored press: to James Franklin and his saucy *New-England Courant* (1721), the third paper in Boston and first to be published without authority; to Benjamin Edes and John Gill and their *Boston Gazette* (founded 1719, first published by them 1755), so outspoken a defender of colonial liberties as to earn from Tories the title of "The Weekly Dung-Barge"; to Andrew Bradford of Philadelphia and the *American Weekly Mercury* (1719), the first paper outside Boston and one much concerned with political liberty; to his nephew William Bradford and the *Pennsylvania Journal* (1741), one of the bravest supporters of the cause of American freedom; to Benjamin Franklin and the *Pennsylvania Gazette* (1729), one of the liveliest and best-written colonial weeklies; to William Parks and the *Maryland Gazette* (1727) and *Virginia Gazette* (1736), the earliest journals in these pivotal colonies; and above all to John Peter Zenger and his *New-York Weekly Journal* (1733). Nor should we forget old Andrew Hamilton of Philadelphia, who appealed to the jury over the heads of a hostile court to win for Zenger a verdict of "not guilty" on a charge of seditious libel. The Zenger trial (1735) is rightly celebrated as an epic of American liberty. Although the principles argued by Hamilton—the admissibility of evidence concerning the truth of an alleged libel and the right of the jury to decide whether a piece of writing is seditious or defamatory—were still many decades from final establishment in law, the release of Zenger was widely acclaimed and did much to put fiber in colonial editors and ginger in their political reporting. Pamphlets and newspapers everywhere printed accounts of the trial, and colonists who had been hitherto indifferent to controversies over liberty and authority discussed it with interest.

The rise of a free press and of a philosophy to defend it is an outstanding example of the manner in which a variety of historical forces combined to bring liberty, independence, and finally democracy to America. Among these may be singled out once again the English descent and interests of the colonists, who drew constantly upon the mother country for political ideas and literary manners; the increase in literacy, learning, and popular desire for news and knowledge, which made widespread printing financially possible; the struggle of factions in the assembly and local governments, which enticed colonial editors into comment on political matters; the fluidity of society and economy, which made it possible for poor but ambitious men like Franklin and Louis Timothée to make a success of printing and publishing; and the increasing recognition among printers and readers that a free press was every man's interest. "THE PRESS," wrote the printer of the *Connecticut Gazette*, "is not so much considered, as the Property of the Men who carry on the Trade of Printing, as of the Publick." And an anonymous correspondent told Zenger, as if he didn't already know:

The *Liberty of the Press* is the *Foundation* of all our other *Liberties*, whether *Civil* or *Religious* and whenever the Liberty of the Press is taken away, either by *open Force*, or any *little, dirty infamous Arts*, we shall immediately become as *wretched*, as *ignorant*, and as *despicable* SLAVES, as any one Nation in all *Europe*.

The muscular press of the Revolution was the gift of a score of independent journeymen, few of whom were aware of the importance of their modest ventures in publishing the news, yet all of whom made a rich contribution to American liberty.

VII

One of the popular slogans of the Revolutionary generation was "a government of laws and not of men." Even the most politically sophisticated American found comfort in this easy formula. The able men of Massachusetts who placed it in their constitution of 1780 knew very well that they, not some words on paper, would govern in the future as they had governed in the past; yet they flattered themselves that they had constructed a political system in which the laws of all generations rather than the discretion of one would be the controlling factor in the conduct of government. By 1765 most colonists believed implicitly that government should be run by men whose status, term of office, duties, powers, and limitations were outlined in organic laws and charters comprehensible to all citizens. Americans counted it a blessing that they were relatively free from the power of magistrates exercising uncontrolled discretion, that they lived under a government prohibited by law from acting out of whim or caprice. As a leader of the North Carolina Regulators wrote, even "if we are all rogues, there must be Law, and all we want is to be Governed by Law, and not by the *Will* of Officers, which to us is perfectly despotick and arbitrary." The colonists not only held to this belief but had institutions to express it. When they thought the mother country had turned to ruling them by whim and caprice, they resisted with the aid of two institutions in particular: written constitutions and standing law.

The American doctrine of a written constitution owes much to England but even more to colonial experience. The state constitutions of 1776-1780 and the federal constitutions of 1778 and 1787 attest the determination of eighteenth-century Americans to live under governments organized, enabled, and limited by written documents. The immediate cause of this flurry of constitution-making was the fact of revolution, which generally compels men who start with a clean slate to fill it up at once with careful directions to their descendants. Yet the virtual unanimity with which politically minded Americans turned to writing constitutions proves that they were acting on principle as well as out of necessity.

It is impossible to locate the exact origins of the American belief in a written constitution. It is possible, however, to point to a half-dozen varieties of fundamental law in colonial times and to suggest that they must have done a great deal to advertise this principle to the awakening American mind.

Whether commercial, proprietary, corporate, or royal, the charter or other basic document of each colony was recognized, however vaguely or grudgingly, as a controlling law. Neither companies, proprietors, nor colonial assemblies had authority to alter the terms of these documents; indeed, a "conformity clause" appeared in one form or other in almost all colonial charters. Self-governing powers were granted the persons or entities named in the charter so long as their "Statutes, Ordinances and Proceedings as near as conveniently may be, be agreeable to the Laws, Statutes, Government, and Policy of this our Realm of England," and colonial lawmakers were therefore concerned to shape their statutes to a higher law. At the same time, the assemblies learned to appeal to the charter and to make capital out of the blessed word "unconstitutional." In some ways the charter was quite different from the modern constitution, but in certain essential features it was itself a constitution, a written, higher, controlling law. The direct line of descent from colonial charter to state constitution is

shown in the fact that the Connecticut charter of
1662 was in force until 1818, the Rhode Island charter
of 1663 until 1842.

Such frustrated or short-lived experiments in English constitution-making as the Agreement of the
People (1647) and the Instrument of Government
(1653) had no more effect on the colonies than they
did on the mother country. English practice and
thought worked upon the American constitutional
tradition in other ways, principally through the
transmission of the great tradition of government
under law and of the habit of devotion and appeal to
Magna Charta and the Bill of Rights. In their insistence upon written constitutions the Revolutionists
were children of the colonial experience; in their
insistence upon constitutionalism they were children
of England.

In Puritan Massachusetts and New Haven, as well
as in other scattered localities that tried consciously
to live by Scripture, the Bible gave a healthy spur to
the belief in a written constitution. The Mosaic Code,
too, was a higher law that men could live by—and
appeal to against the decrees and whims of ordinary
men.

America's debt to the idea of the social contract is
so huge as to defy measurement, and we should not
forget that the colonists had a unique opportunity
—or so at least they thought—to put the idea into
practice. Such written expressions of this ancient
doctrine as the Mayflower Compact (1620) and the
Fundamental Orders of Connecticut (1639) were
primitive exercises in constitution-making in which
the colonists themselves engaged. We must be careful, however, not to regard these as constitutions in
our sense of the word.

The articles of association of many of the separatist
or other dissenting churches were a special type of

compact or agreement. In areas where church organization had a pronounced effect upon civil government, the covenant did much to encourage the tradition and practices of constitutionalism. Nor should it be forgotten that rules of conduct and mutual assistance adopted by groups of these churches—for example, the Platform of Church Discipline accepted at Cambridge in 1649—assumed with the passing of the years those characteristics of sanctity and untouchability which add so much to the influence of our modern constitutions.

Finally, we ought not overlook the plans of government bestowed upon certain colonies by their well-meaning sponsors. Some of these were miserable failures, notably John Locke's grandiose Fundamental Constitutions of Carolina; some were reasonably successful experiments, notably William Penn's Frames of Government. All were ancestors of our modern constitutions.

A final point should be made about these forerunners of the American constitutions: Not only were they written, higher, and sacred, and in some sense controlling law; not only did they stimulate the principles and habits of constitutionalism; but most of them included a grant or acknowledgment of individual liberties, immunities, or privileges. The assumption that no constitution is complete unless it incorporates a specific bill of rights may also be traced back through colonial experience to the English past.

The growth of standing law in the colonies did much to give practical content to the slogan "a government of laws and not of men." By the middle of the eighteenth century the relations of man to man and of man to community were governed almost everywhere by codes, statutes, and established principles that were known, certain, comprehensible, and to a large extent equal in application. Just as the written constitution was designed primarily to limit the whim of executive and legislature, so the standing law served primarily to regularize the procedures and punishments of the judiciary and its agents. The history of law and courts in colonial times is largely one of the steady reduction of judicial discretion to limits consistent with the dictates of free government. In this instance in particular, the advance from primitive diversity to mature uniformity was marked by an increase in individual liberty.

Popular demand for standing law was as old as the colonies. As early as 1618 in Virginia, 1641 in Massachusetts, 1647 in Rhode Island, 1650 in Connecticut, and 1656 in New Haven, codes of laws based on experience and English usage had been enacted in response to popular demand. As other colonies were founded, the inhabitants of these, too, were quick to seek procedural guaranties in codes, statutes, and fundamental orders. And in all colonies, old and new, the standing law was sporadically revised and elaborated by assemblies and courts.

The law of seventeenth-century America was simple, practical, and primitive. The magistrates retained an unusual degree of discretion, but they exercised this discretion in keeping with the mores and needs of the homogeneous community. Justice was rough and ready, but so was society. The common law had little influence either in detail or general principle, except in such colonies as New York, where the homogeneity of other colonies was lacking, and Maryland, which made a special effort to import elements of the English system. One reason for the lack of influence of the common law was the active prejudice against lawyers and consequent amateurism of bench and bar.

In the eighteenth century the common law was imported into American jurisprudence on a large scale. Among the reasons for this turn of events were the growing maturity and complexity of the settled regions, the increase in imperial control, and the development of a trained bench and bar. It was natural for lawyers and judges, many of whom had been educated at the Inns of Court in London, to turn to to the mighty reservoir of legal experience in their own language. By the middle of the century the standing law in America was a unique amalgam of elements drawn from colonial experience and English precedent. In one sense, the importation of the property-conscious common law was a triumph for conservatism or even reaction. In other ways, however, it furthered the cause of liberty and democracy. The common law helped reinvigorate that "sturdy sense of right" inherited from the mother country; it became, through the appeal to its liberating features, a synonym for liberty and thus a weapon of the Revolutionists; and it trained a whole generation of patriots like Jefferson and John Adams. Burke was sure that the "untractable spirit" of the Americans could be traced to the fact that "in no country perhaps in the world is the law so general a study." The rights of Englishmen were soon to become the rights of all men, and of these none was more precious than to live and do business under a standing law.

Several important details of organization and philosophy were missing in 1765 from the American doctrines of constitutionalism and the rule of law. The constitutional convention, popular ratification, judicial review, and "constitution-worship" were not yet incorporated into the belief in a written constitution. The writ of habeas corpus and other common-law liberties were secured in most colonies only by imported precedents and the willingness of judges and magistrates to follow them. But the spirit of constitutionalism was fixed in the colonial mind. Americans were becoming ever more attached to the conviction that free government demands a high level of political morality, that political morality is best expressed through constitutional procedures, and that constitutionalism is therefore not only a product but a prerequisite of freedom. The American democracy, like all true democracies, has been pre-eminently a *constitutional* democracy. The transfer of the ancient tenets of English constitutionalism to the colonies was therefore a memorable stage of American liberty.

For the most part, of course, the colonists had their political sights set a good deal lower than these lofty notions of law and constitutionalism. Most of them seem to have been too concerned with problems of existence to give much thought or energy to problems of government. The mass of men went about their business quite indifferent to issues and elections, cultivating in their own nonpolitical ways those attitudes of liberty, justice, and individualism which were to stand them in good stead in the era of the Revolution. The minority that was enfranchised and attentive to public affairs pursued the politics of freedom on a limited stage. Whatever political democracy did exist was a democracy of white male property owners.

Yet the fact remains that these people, though they were chiefly concerned with their own short-range interests and had no intention of sharing political power with the disqualified majority, made use of institutions and arguments that were to prove readily convertible to democratic purposes. Their institutions were elective, representative, secular, constitutional, and limited by law; their arguments were framed in terms of "liberty" and "the people." When to these elements were finally added an expanded suffrage and a belief in the political capacity of the average man, the triumph of political democracy was secure. The groundwork of this triumph was laid in the colonial period. Before there could be democracy there had to be liberty and self-government, and before Washington could make his revolution the men of the assemblies had to make theirs.

V

Better Sort, Middling Sort, Meaner Sort: The Structure of Colonial Society

The sociology of the American settlements is a subject to which increasing numbers of colonial historians now devote their talents for tireless probing and prudent reconstruction. In recent years we have learned a great deal we had only guessed at before about social problems in colonial times. We have learned, too, of the profound influence of social attitudes on the evolution of self-government and of a democratic faith.

Social problems and attitudes are the concern of this chapter. I shall confine it to a hard core of sociological topics, placing emphasis as usual on their significance for the rise of political liberty: the class structure of the colonies; the units of social organization—family, farm, plantation, town, and city; certain problems common to all societies, such as crime and punishment, status of women and children, and care of the unfortunate; and, once again, those broad social developments which made it possible for the colonists to think, act, and ultimately fight in terms of human liberty. In each of the preliminary chapters I discussed questions that might easily have been included under this heading: in Chapter I, the racial and national origins of the people of the colonies; in Chapter II, the economic forces that helped shape society; in Chapter III, a variety of problems of individual belief and group behavior in an age when many men considered their religion a way of life; in Chapter IV, political behavior, especially the extent of popular participation in politics. And we have yet to examine, in Chapter VI, the influence of the social structure of the colonies on the instruments and ideals of education and culture.

I

Each of the colonies exhibited a class structure more fully developed and generally acknowledged than any we could imagine in modern America. In some areas classes existed from the first settlement; in others they developed from an original condition of near-equality under circumstances that favored the growth of social divisions. Two circumstances in particular led to the formation of classes: the influence of a frontier economy, above all the fact that land and profits could be obtained by different men in grossly different quantities; and the inheritance from England and Europe of a tradition of social stratification. While the class structure was not so rigid as that of England or Germany, it was well-defined enough to work a determining influence on politics, education, and culture.

To define a class and distinguish it from other classes is no simple matter, especially in a pioneer society. Yet the thinking colonist, had he been asked about the "ranks" and "sorts" of people in his own experience, could have pointed with some accuracy to five separate classes of men who passed daily before his eyes: the "better sort," which in some times and places was merely the top class on the ladder but in others was a genuine colonial aristocracy made up of large landholders, crown officials, merchants, and allied lawyers and professional men; the "middling sort," the numerous body of small landholders, independent artisans, shopkeepers, petty officials, and professional

men of lesser pretensions; the "meaner sort," the free
but depressed category of poor men who were laborers, servants, dependent artisans, sailors, unprosperous
farmers, and nondescript drifters; the bonded white
servants, an even meaner sort, who served some master under an indenture limited in time; and the very
lowest elements of society, the Negroes, of whom
only a few thousand had been delivered from the
curse of bondage into a precarious condition of legal
freedom. All these strata of men had an immense influence on the development of the colonies, but only
the first two took an active part in the ferment-
ing process of self-government. Wealth, occupation,
learning, ancestry, religion, national origin, breeding,
and pretensions were the ingredients of class distinction, and as always in America wealth and pretensions
led all the rest. Then as now the only poor folk in the
upper class were elderly ladies whose grandfathers had
been governors of South Carolina.

Popular belief in the existence of a better sort—distinguishable from ordinary men by dress, bearing, and
speech, and entitled to leadership, respect, and even
deference—prevailed almost everywhere throughout
the colonial period. In 1636 the ruling elders of Massachusetts Bay agreed with Lord Say and Sele that the
politically active community "should consist of two
distinct ranks of men"—"gentlemen of the country"
and "freeholders." In 1651 the General Court of Massachusetts declared its "vtter detestation & dislike
that men or women of meane condition . . . should
take vppon them the garbe of gentlemen, by the
wearing of golde or silver lace, or buttons." In 1674
a tailor in York County, Virginia, was punished for
racing a horse, since "it was contrary to law for a la-
bourer to make a race, being a sport only for gentlemen." In the eighteenth century both Harvard and
Yale used "family dignity" as the chief criterion in
"placing" each student in his class. And in 1775 the

revolutionary Virginia Convention resolved that "the natural strength, and only security of a free government" was "a well regulated militia, composed of Gentlemen and Yeomen." These official opinions were echoed in thousands of letters, diaries, newspaper articles, and books in which authors expressed or implied a belief in the gentry and its right to lead. Who were these gentlemen who dominated the social, economic, and political life of every colony?

The New England aristocracy of the eighteenth century was for the most part the product of an expanding commercial capitalism. The leading members of the upper class were the wealthy merchants, around whose central position revolved their lawyers, their ministers, and an occasional master artisan or shopkeeper of impeccable lineage. Only in Rhode Island was there an upper class chiefly dependent on extensive holdings of land for its wealth and status. The Narragansett Planters, with their stock-producing plantations, gangs of Negro slaves, fast and famous horses, and orthodox Church-of-England opinions, were a fascinating variant from the normal social pattern. In Massachusetts and New Hampshire there was frosting on the cake in the person of the royal governor, his devoted retinue of officials, and those merchants who displayed an abnormal desire to be classed as English gentry. Only in Boston, where reigned the Hutchinsons, Olivers, Faneuils, Hancocks, Amorys, Boylstons, and Lechmeres, and in Newport, where reigned (and slaved) the Redwoods, Eastons, Wantons, Bernons, Malbones, Ellerys, Paines, Ayraults, and Brinleys, did capital accumulation, polite manners, and the uses of conspicuous wealth reach proportions that permitted the favored few to behave and think like true American aristocrats. Daniel West, an English visitor to Boston in 1720, acknowledged "that a gentleman from London would almost think himself at home at Boston, when he observes the number of

people, their houses, their furniture, their tables,
their dress and conversation, which perhaps is as splen-
did and showy as that of the most considerable
tradesmen in London"—about as decent a compliment
as an Englishman could pay to an upper class still actively concerned with the sources of its wealth. The
wealthy merchants of Portsmouth, Salem, Providence,
New Haven, and a half-dozen lesser ports could also
be classed as a native aristocracy, but in hundreds of
New England towns the better sort occupied a position not too far above that of the celebrated yeomen.

The middle colonies harbored two remarkable aristocracies. In New York, perhaps the most stratified
of all thirteen colonies, an authentic aristocracy grew
quickly out of the maldistribution of land. Schuyler,
De Lancey, Livingston, Beekman, Philipse, Lloyd, Van
Cortlandt, Smith, Heathcote, Morris, and Van Rens-
selaer were the names of the most prominent landholding families. As the colony developed, members
of these powerful clans joined Crugers, Van Horns,
Van Dams, Floyds, Bayards, and Waltons in the city
in wringing profits and leisure from commerce and
the law. In the meantime, merchant families sought
additional wealth and prestige by acquiring landed es-
tates. A politically important characteristic of the
New York aristocracy was the fantastic pattern of
intermarriage among leading families. When Abram
De Peyster died in 1767, Van Cortlandts, De Lanceys,
Beekmans, Livingstons, Schuylers, Jays, Philipses, and
many other aristocratic families crowded the church
to see their relative off to Heaven. Cadwallader Colden, in recommending to the Board of Trade that
Judge Robert R. Livingston be removed from judicial
office, pointed out that "no Cause of any Consequence can come before him in which . . . he or the
Livingston Family are not interested." No aristocracy
dominated all phases of a colony's affairs so completely
as did these children of England, Holland, and France.

They ruled with condescension, lived in splendor, and got the deference that was their due.

Philadelphia's aristocracy was commercial in character. Norrises, Shippens, Pembertons, Hills, Logans, Carpenters, Dickinsons, and Merediths were some of the solid Quaker families with which other non-Quaker families allied themselves as the city progressed toward its pre-Revolutionary peak of culture and urbanity. The persistence of inherited notions of social stratification is most clearly visible in the social attitudes of the wealthy Quakers, who rarely preached or practiced egalitarianism. Here in Philadelphia, too, was exhibited most ridiculously that peculiar trait of our peculiar aristocracy: Consisting entirely of children and grandchildren of self-made men, the upper class looked upon self-made men of its own generation with a contempt that would have done credit to a Spanish grandee.

In the South flourished the most memorable of provincial aristocracies. However disparate their English origins, the planters of eighteenth-century Virginia—Carters, Byrds, Lees, Corbins, Randolphs, Fitzhughs, Beverleys, Blairs, Blands, Masons, and Pages—formed a self-conscious aristocracy that derived its status from the land and ruled in the Whig tradition. Cheap and exploitable land, a plentiful supply of slaves, and an easily grown staple were the economic supports of the Virginia aristocracy. The first gentlemen of Maryland—Tilghmans, Darnalls, Carrolls, Ringgolds, Snowdens, Addisons, Dulanys, Taskers, Goldsboroughs —were hardly less eminent; the first gentlemen of South Carolina—Pinckneys, Draytons, Middletons, Manigaults, Izards, Rutledges, Ravenels, Bees, and Hugers—were if anything more cultivated, haughty, and jealous of their privileges. Charleston was to South Carolina what New York City was to the Hudson Valley: the focal point of culture of an aristocracy with interests in both commerce and land.

Slavery, the Anglican Church, and close social and economic ties with England gave the upper class in the South a special feeling that it was a genuine aristocracy, one that in Eliza Pinckney's words lived "very Gentile and very much in the English taste."

Throughout the colonies, but especially north of Maryland, a class of families who considered themselves neither "mean" nor "gentle" increased and multiplied. These were the self-respecting ancestors of the great middle class to which some 80 to 90 per cent of the American people now profess to belong. Up from this class had climbed hundreds of the proudest families of the aristocracy, and up to it climbed, especially in prosperous times, thousands upon thousands of former servants, laborers, and other unpropertied men. The middling sort flourished alike on the farm or in the city. This was particularly true of New England, New Jersey, and Pennsylvania, the happy lands of the colonial middle class. The hard-working, self-reliant, property-conscious farmers of Essex, Fairfield, Bergen, and Bucks counties found their social and political equals in the hard-working, self-reliant, property-conscious shopkeepers and independent artisans of Boston, New London, Burlington, and Philadelphia.

In New York and the Southern colonies the middling sort lacked the numbers, secure status, and influence they enjoyed in Pennsylvania and New England. The land policies of the aristocracy in New York and the cruel sway of slavery and soil exhaustion in Virginia and South Carolina made the sturdy yeoman a much rarer bird in those highly stratified colonies than was good for their economic and social health. Yet the social pyramid showed a layer between the upper and lower classes: Small farms and freeholds dotted the map of New York; overseers and factors performed important functions in the Southern colonies; many yeomen refused to be driven out or depressed in Virginia; artisans and small tradesmen offered their services in New York, Norfolk, Charleston, Wilmington, and Baltimore; and out into the Piedmont and the valleys of the west streamed thousands who had no hope of being gentle and no intention of being mean.

The free white man with too little property or no property at all could be found in most professions and all colonies. He was most likely to be a tiller of the soil, which was often his own and as often some other man's. Most tenants and all farm laborers were members of the lower class. The line between the middling and inferior freeholder was drawn by each community in terms of property and stability. In every New England town or Southern parish there were prosperous yeomen fixed in the middle class and grubbing peasants fixed in the lower. Between these two groups swung a mass of farmers whom bad times made "mean" and good times "middling." Since the prosperous middling farmers were fully conscious of their status and political rights, this third group was generally classed as "mean." The line between the middle and lower class was more sharply drawn in the city or large village, where occupation and economic independence had more to do with a man's position. Dependent artisans, free servants, laborers, sailors, and apprentices made up the meaner sort in Boston, New York, and Philadelphia.

Good times or bad, in country or in city, thousands of free whites were anchored permanently in the lower class. These were the men who lacked the intelligence, luck, or perseverance to set up shop for themselves or to acquire and work successfully the land that was theirs for the asking. Only in the South, where many a capable person was ground between the upper stone of the planters and the lower of Negro slavery, was the man of the lower class more likely to be the victim of circumstance rather than of his own shortcomings. A good portion of the meaner sort was the residue of those dregs of English society transported under bond or court order to the colonies.

At one time or another in the colonial period more than a quarter of a million persons were placed willingly or unwillingly in the status known as indentured servitude. This status was a species of semislavery limited in time (four to seven years) by contract and in severity by the European rather than African origin of the bonded man or woman. The indentured servant had, in effect, sold a number of years of labor in return for passage across the sea and the promise of certain benefits at the time of release. Most men and women of this class were bound before their departure to masters in America or to a ship captain or agent who would sell them and their contract upon arrival. A large number, particularly among the German families of Pennsylvania, came as "redemptioners" or "free-willers," with a chance to find a friend or relative to pay their passage before being turned back to the ship captain for auction to the highest bidder. A healthy fraction of the indentured class was in it willy-nilly: convicts, felons, and kidnaped persons, as well as debtors and other social unfortunates already in the colonies. The indentured white might serve in any capacity, even that of schoolmaster, but generally he was a farm hand or domestic servant.

Indentured servitude flourished most vigorously in seventeenth-century Virginia and Maryland and in eighteenth-century Pennsylvania. In Virginia in 1683 fully one-sixth of the population was passing through the state of servitude. Almost two-thirds of the immigrants to Pennsylvania in the eighteenth century were indentured whites. New England, suspicious of strangers and incapable of employing them in large numbers, received comparatively few of this class of men. South of New England, where cheap labor was an absorbing need, more than one-half of all persons who migrated to the colonies were indentured servants.

The indentured servant's lot was rough but endurable. Unlike the Negro slave, he was not completely dependent on the character of his master, for he had legal and property rights—and he was a white Christian. The age was one in which men were not unaccustomed to the notion of selling themselves or being sold. Indentured servitude was simply the English system of binding out the poor, young, and unemployed, reshaped to the insatiable needs of a frontier economy. Degraded men who entered or were forced into servitude were all the more degraded by this experience, but thousands of respectable Englishmen, Germans, and Scotch-Irish passed through servitude to liberty and often on to prosperity without loss of self-respect. Peter Kalm reported that many Germans in Pennsylvania preferred temporary bondage in order to learn the language and customs of the country and to "better be able to consider what they shall do when they have got their liberty." It would be pleasant to confirm the popular assumption that most indentured servants went on to become sturdy yeomen and independent artisans, but the harsh fact is, as A. E. Smith has proved conclusively, that only a small fraction ever rose into the middle class. Most of these people were of humble origin, and most of them turned to humble occupations upon achieving their freedom. South of Connecticut the "meaner sort" were for the most part former bondsmen or convicts who had served their time. The vicious character of the time-serving convicts, the rise of a strong aristocracy, and the corrupting influence of slavery all contributed to the decline in status of the servant class in the later decades of the colonial period.

Lowest of the social classes were the Negro slaves. Some idea of the importance of this miserable order

of unwilling captives may be drawn from the estimated census of 1765: 1,450,000 whites, 400,000 Negroes. All but a tiny fraction of the latter were chat-
tel slaves, fully seven-eighths of them living in the
five southernmost colonies. In South Carolina they
outnumbered the white population by two to one.
And even in the North, especially in New York,
Rhode Island, and Connecticut, they were counted
in thousands. Slavery existed in law and fact in each
of the thirteen colonies.

Negro slavery was the social product of many powerful forces: the search for cheap labor by an economy
devoted to the wasteful production of tobacco, rice,
and indigo; the desire of slaver and planter for profits
and more profits; the mores and traditions of a cold-
blooded age; and the crude facts that the Negro was
strong, black, and primitive, though hardly more
primitive than many poor whites. Slavery was not
immediately established with the landing of the first
Negroes but developed in response to circumstances
of place and time. The social position of the Negro, if
it can be called that, grew worse rather than better
as the Southern colonies expanded and prospered.

Few white colonists ever regarded the Negro as
even a very inferior and unfortunate brother. Most
men were indifferent to his problems or fate, assum-
ing that if and when freed he and his fellows would
naturally constitute the lowest class. Only among the
poor whites of the South was there a well-defined
class attitude toward the Negro; and, as might be expected in an essentially competitive situation, it was
one of veiled hostility or vicious hatred. The general
colonial attitude toward slaves and slavery was essentially this: Until the very days of the Revolution few
white men, even the most sincere friends of liberty,
thought it anything but "natural" that such a condition should exist. The mental climate of the colonies
was overwhelmingly hostile to the assumption that

the Negro was a whole man. Advertisements hawking "several negro Girls and a negro Boy, and likewise good Cheshire Cheese" ran in the newspapers constantly. Only in Pennsylvania and certain parts of rural New England did the Negro, slave or free, enjoy reasonably normal and intimate contacts with the white man. As a result, most speculation about natural rights and equality simply ignored the Negro. Evidence of this social attitude was the restricted and degraded life led by the free Negro, even in New England.

The influence of slavery on colonial society was terrible in consequence. If slavery helped the Southern colonies to develop much faster than might otherwise have been expected, its total effect was a distressing catalogue of social ills: It exalted a few whites, degraded many more, permitted sinfully wasteful agriculture, created a miasma of fear in areas where Negroes were plentiful, hardened class lines, stunted the growth of the Southern middle class, cheapened respect for labor, and dehumanized man's sympathy for man in an age already inhuman enough. As for the slave himself, the sin against him was so colossal as to give most Americans the chills even to this day. The specious argument that the Negro was better off as a slave until he could be raised to the minimal standards of the white man's civilization was undercut by colonial laws that made slaves of the children of slaves. Neither economically nor spiritually was slavery seriously challenged at any time in the colonial period. There was no place for the Negro in the American definition of the rights of man.

In conclusion, these characteristics of the class structure provide convincing evidence that the America of 1765 had moved much farther into the future than had the countries left behind: the indigenous and severely functional nature of the several classes, which were as much the creation of the American environment as of the European heritage; the evolving content of the criteria of class distinctions, in which personal achievement loomed ever more important; the fluidity of membership in each class, with the Negro alone anchored permanently in his status; the softening of the twin attitudes of condescension and deference; and the relatively strong feeling of social solidarity, thanks to an expanding middle class and a rising standard of living. The colonists, to be sure, continued to accept the notion of social classes without qualm or question, but this old-world legacy had been tempered considerably by a new-world insistence that every man should rise or fall by his own virtues and capacities. Then as now Americans assumed that an open-ended class structure was wholly compatible with constitutional government and personal liberty.

II

It is hard for modern Americans to realize how dominant a role the family played in the lives of their colonial ancestors. Tradition, circumstance, and law united to give the family a prime responsibility for the functioning of society. In response to the burdens thrust upon it, the colonial family was highly patriarchal in organization. The head of the family, however kindly, was a near-absolute master within the unit; at the same time, he was its exclusive representative to the larger community in political, economic, and religious affairs. The family not only incorporated parents, children, and all manner of dependent relatives, but also included free and bonded servants, slaves, and boarders. An average family might easily number thirty people. Few were the colonists who would or could "live alone and like it." Indeed, "the selfish luxury of solitary living" was looked upon with suspicion. In early New England, law and custom made life particularly uncomfortable for the unmarried and unattached man or woman. A New Haven law of 1656 ordered:

That no single person of either Sex, do henceforward board, diet, or Sojourn, or be permitted to do so, or to have lodging; or house room within any of the Plantations of this Jurisdiction, but either in some allowed Relation, or in some approved Family licensed thereunto. . . . The Governor of which Family, so licensed, shal as he may conveniently, duly observe the course, carriage, and behaviour, of every such single person, whether he, or she walk diligently in a constant imployment, attending both Family duties, and the publick worship of God, and keeping good order day and night, or otherwise.

As for the South, Colonel Byrd wrote that "an Old Maid or an Old Bachelor are as scarce among us and reckoned as ominous as a Blazing Star." The often ludicrous haste with which widows and widowers sought remarriage attests to the intrinsic nature of the family tie.

The family served society in a half-dozen essential capacities. It was the key agency of human association, the leading instrument of education, and an important secondary center of religious life and instruction. In addition, whether occupied primarily in farm or shop, it was a virtually self-sustaining economic unit and, in its developed stage, the leading producer of food and manufactured articles. The influence of the family upon society at large was visited forcefully upon the field of politics. Its focal position made the father a special person in the eyes of the world and thus helped justify the fact of limited suffrage. The family was a principal agent in diffusing those virtues out of which colonists thought the good society would arise: industry, frugality, humility, piety, honesty, charity, and that famous American blend of self-reliance and communal spirit. And finally, it was a powerful force for social stability in a society that was becoming progressively more "open."

Although the family was the cell of three larger forms of social organization—plantation, town, and city—it also existed as a self-contained unit, with no buffer except a poorly organized county between it and the colony. This was especially true of the family engaged in limited and freehold farming in the South in the seventeenth century and almost everywhere outside settled New England in the eighteenth. The consuming purpose of families in this category was plain: to farm for subsistence and if possible for exchange. To this paramount task each member of the family contributed his efforts. Few American farms had even a single hired man or bonded servant. The only person to have contact with the larger world— and he only rarely—was the father. The family itself lived, loved, suffered, and toiled in a state of isolation almost impossible to comprehend. Thousands of families were denied even the occasional diversions of a crossroads settlement or a church.

The social attitudes generated by this life of narrow toil and isolation were understandably mixed. Certainly it encouraged crudity, ignorance, slovenliness, immorality, violence, shiftlessness, and parochialism; yet fierce independence, lack of concern for social standing, voluntary co-operation, and inquisitive friendliness to strangers were other qualities the open country bred more generously than the built-up settlement. And the gathering resentments harbored by this class of men—who were often in debt, underrepresented or ignored in the developing process of self-government, plagued by rents and taxes, and exposed without support to the ravages of Indian warfare— hastened the coming of real democracy.

The rural isolation of the farm was matched by that of the plantation, but in most other particulars the latter was a quite different type of social institution. Here the family was the center of a group that might easily number fifty to one hundred relatives, tenants, hired workers, and slaves. The line between the large farm and small plantation was often difficult to trace, but there was no mistaking the true plantation. Some of its distinguishing marks were: a large tract of land; an economic pattern on one hand quite self-contained, on the other devoted to growing a staple for export; a numerous and servile working force; a master and mistress who worked hard but avoided menial labor; and a family that strove consciously to live in gentle style, importing many of its props and ideas from England.

The plantation family refused to be provincialized by its distance from other plantations and from centers of population and culture. Its members, especially the head, were a hundred times more mobile than the poor farming family. An area of plantations therefore produced a more sociable, cultivated, worldly, and public-spirited class of men than an area of small and struggling farms. One of the consuming purposes of the planter was to make it possible for his children to live on the same high level he had occupied. He therefore spent considerable time finding proper husbands for his daughters and adequate lands for his sons. This attitude of class consciousness and social aspiration distinguished the planter from the lesser men about him. The colonial plantation, whether devoted to indigo in Georgia, rice in the Carolinas, tobacco in Virginia and Maryland, or stock raising in southwestern Rhode Island, was the fertile nursery of America's landed aristocracy. The New York manor, an overextended rural unit built on tenantry rather than slavery, also produced a ruling attitude of caste, culture, and conservatism.

The New England town was the most highly developed unit of communal organization in the colonies. Like most early American institutions it was a product of the interaction of an English inheritance and a wilderness environment. In the close-knit settlements of

New England, and in their early offshoots in New York and New Jersey, the family joined with other families of like mind and purpose in a planned pattern of community living quite removed from that of the Southern colonies. We have already examined or will examine shortly the techniques through which the men of the towns achieved their common ends in politics, land distribution, religion, and education. In each of these matters they placed constant emphasis on the larger purposes of the community rather than the wishes or whims of the individual. A newcomer or would-be purchaser had to meet the standards of the community before he could settle in a New England or Long Island town. The records are full of entries like these:

It is ordered yt whosoever shall take up a lot in Towne shal live upon it himselfe and also yt no man shal sell his alotment or any part thereof unless it be to such as ye Towne shall aprove of and give consent to ye sale thereof.

It is ordered that Daniel Turner shall within the space of ffortnite eythe sojurne in some ffamily or bee a servant to some or else Depart the towne.

at a towne meeting the 6th of June 1664 it was voted and agreed by the magar vot that Jery Wood shall have liberty to perchas heare in this towne and to be reseved as an inhabitante.

The townsman was made constantly aware that he could enjoy his measure of freedom only as part of a more important whole:

at a towne meeting it was voeted and agread vpon that the fence be maed vp at the end of the ould feeld fence and thay that doe not com to help about it the next Thursday every man that is wanting shall pay five shillens.

He was permitted isolation or eccentricity in many affairs that we would find important, but in all matters of vital concern to the community he was asked for public service and for conformity in thought and action. The social result was a mixture of individualism and communal feeling that boded well for the democratic future. The town resolved the conflicting claims of liberty and authority more sensibly than any other institution in colonial America. If it bred provincialism, it also bred ordered liberty.

A famous son of a famous town explained why New Englanders found New England superior to "every other colony in America and, indeed, of every other part of the world that I know anything of":

> In all countries and in all companies, for several years, I have, in conversation and in writing, enumerated the towns, militia, schools, and churches, as the four causes of the growth and defence of New England. The virtues and talents of the people are there formed; their temperance, patience, fortitude, prudence, and justice, as well as their sagacity, knowledge, judgment, taste, skill, ingenuity, dexterity, and industry.

Adams spoke as advocate for his section and way of life, yet his rendering of the causes of New England's unusual measure of stability, solidarity, and well-being was essentially sound. He might have mentioned other influences: the tavern, which rivaled the church and town meeting as a centripetal force; the developing highway system, which made it possible for the family far from the main part of town to discharge its political, religious, and social duties; the twin institutions of "inhabitancy" and "warning-out"; and the unusual proportion of people who could be classed as the middling sort. Far more significant politically than the silly notions and rules of stratification entertained in many towns was the profound leveling effect of small landholdings and a stable way of life. Thanks to the town and to the habits and virtues it rewarded, New England was the first great home of the American middle class.

Five concentrations of population, all of them seaports, could be classed as cities in 1765: Boston (15,-

500), Newport (8,000), New York (18,000), Philadelphia (30,000), and Charleston (10,000). In addition, such ports as Salem, Portsmouth, Providence, New Haven, New London, Perth Amboy, Annapolis, Baltimore, Norfolk, Wilmington, and Savannah, and such country towns as Lynn, Hartford, Albany, Burlington, Princeton, Lancaster, Germantown, and Williamsburg had taken on some of the characteristics of urban living. These cities and large settlements had an influence out of all proportion to their population on the struggle for an open society, self-government, an independent economy, social maturity, and an American culture.

The growth of an indigenous class structure was hastened by circumstances of urban living. The city environment was especially favorable to the rise of an aristocracy. Profits could be made more quickly and reinvested more imaginatively; occupation, thanks to specialization of labor, was a more definite criterion of status; and the gentle pleasures, whether of the club or the dancing class, could be pursued without excessive effort and in any season. Conditions also favored the firm establishment of a shopkeeping middle class and laboring lower class. Yet the class structure, if more visible than that of the country, was at the same time more fluid. Men in the bustling city moved up and down the ladder more rapidly than men in the conservative country.

Popular participation and public interest in political affairs were much keener in urban than in rural areas. Here in the city were the visible instruments of provincial government: the chambers of the assembly and the residence of the governor. Here, too, was the home of the printing press, that new engine of politics. Where participation lagged, as in tightly run Philadelphia and badly governed Charleston, interest was kept alive by the club, tavern, weekly, pamphlet, broadside, and public concourse. Internecine warfare among the established classes brought the lower orders ever nearer to political emancipation.

The city was the narrow throat of the main streams of commerce that flowed to and from the productive American land, and as such it led the way toward an ever more bountiful, rewarding, and freewheeling economy. The economic pattern of the city was diverse and fast-moving; it held out opportunities to the industrious and frugal man that could not be surpassed anywhere in the Atlantic community. The momentous clash between the old world of mercantilism and new world of economic individualism was largely decided in the colonial cities.

The city came to grips long before the country with the problems of a growing society. It was forced by necessity to take public action and use public funds in such matters as care of the poor, punishment of crime, regulation of markets, and prevention of fire. At the same time, the men of the city learned that private initiative and voluntary action were likewise workable methods for solving common problems. The association of free men for social, economic, and political purposes got its first real test in Boston and Philadelphia. While the country remained in a condition of social infancy, the city pushed upward, thanks to men like Franklin, toward new levels of communal co-operation.

Finally, the city was the crucible of a new culture. The grand cultural achievement of the colonial age, the reception and conversion of English and European tastes and ideas, was largely the work of the upper and middle classes in the cities. Education, literature, science, and the arts flourished most vigorously in the cities. At the same time, an influential process of cultural exchange went on among the leading seaports. Carl Bridenbaugh writes that by the 1740's "it was possible for an educated gentleman like Dr. Alexander Hamilton to travel the length of the colonies with

letters in his pocket to the cultural leaders in each
community, to converse and exchange ideas with
them, and enter into discussions, activities and amuse-
ments. Nothing better indicates the emergence of a
definite urban society." Nothing better indicates the
emergence of centers of social and economic power
that would provide the necessary leadership in the
pre-Revolutionary decade. Boston rather than Lexington and Concord led the way to independence.

III

Most colonists shared a common set of assumptions
and prejudices about such matters as the status of
women and care of the unfortunate. A review of the
colonial approach to problems found in all societies
will lead to several conclusions about the level of social consciousness in these pioneering communities.

In law, custom, and practice colonial women occupied a position well below the status of near-equality
enjoyed by women in modern America. The common
law subjected both the person and property of a married woman to her husband's control; and since the
pressures of colonial society forced most women to
marry young and stay married, the law as inherited
and applied recognized two different ranks of people.
Women played no part in government and only a
small part in business. Except for the brave widow
who carried on with her late husband's shop, inn,
press, or plantation, woman's place was by the hearth.
The fact of male social and legal superiority was rationalized by the assumption of female intellectual
inferiority. Education for women was elementary and,
except among the better sort, wholly utilitarian.

Their value as wives, housekeepers, and mothers
was, of course, recognized by all. The institution of
marriage was held in high esteem. Indeed, in a society

with too many men and with laws forbidding bonded men to marry, the marital tie was a badge of respectability. Once married and settled in her new home, the wife entered upon a regimen of labor that would appall modern woman. In middle-class and lower-class homes she was cook, baker, nurse, teacher, seamstress, laundress, and manager of the economy. Wives of poor farmers devoted their odd hours to the fields. In the upper-class home the wife was more manager than doer. The mistress of the plantation was perhaps the most responsible and hard-working woman in the colonies. Women in all stations were, as an English nobleman observed, "in general great Breeders." Whether the help her children gave her compensated for the hardship of bearing and raising them is a question on which no colonial woman has left any clear testimony. Toil and parturition were her lot, yet she was not heard to complain any louder than modern woman. Unaware that her descendants would have waffle irons and anesthesia, she got along surprisingly well without the comforts that even husbands consider the basic necessities of modern women.

The status of women improved slowly but measurably throughout the colonial period. If they did not attain anything like equality with men, they nevertheless won—thanks principally to their scarcity— more respect, freedom, and legal recognition than their sisters in England and Europe. Conditions made it possible for many women, especially former indentured servants, to marry well above them. In many colonies the legal rights or capacities of women in property, conveyance of land, marriage and divorce, inheritance, contracts, torts, and testimony were expanded well beyond the reactionary confines of the common law. And everywhere, as many a traveler attested, they enjoyed a measure of freedom in coming and going that set older women to shaking their heads. This improvement in status was an inevitable result of the enhanced bargaining power bestowed on women by a surplus of men.

The total contribution of women to the development of the colonies has never been adequately acknowledged, except by women historians. Not only did they labor at a hundred essential tasks that men would not or could not perform, not only did they procreate the race with unexampled fertility, but they acted as a powerful stabilizing influence in the evolution of society. Violence, religious primitivism, alcoholism, and shiftlessness were noticeably less prevalent in those areas where settled homes and decent women were most numerous. The women of colonial America were inferior in status but not in influence.

The status of children was comparable to that of their mothers: They might be loved and cherished, but they were clearly more subject to discipline and authority than children of later times. Obedience without question was the cardinal virtue in colonial children. I shall take notice in Chapter VI of the poverty and practicality of their education, which was shaped by the plain economic truth that they were valued highly for the assistance they could bring the family, even at an early age—the boys as helpers in field, barn, woodshed, and shop, the girls as comforts to overworked mothers. And if there were no place for them in the home economy, they could be bound out as apprentices. In general, what was true of women was true of children: They were subject to the command of the master of the house, finding scant refuge from severity or cruelty in either law or custom; they were welcomed particularly for their contributions of an economic nature; and they endured an existence that to us seems unbelievably hard and cruel, yet to them, in an age of limited knowledge and horizons, must have seemed about as secure and happy as a child's life today. Children giggled and mooned, socialized and withdrew, laughed and cried in those days, too.

The criminal record of the colonies was better than might have been expected of a frontier society that had inherited some of the more vicious notions and people of the parent country. Convictions for arson, rape, robbery, infanticide, murder, and other crimes are to be found in the records of every colonial court, but life and property seem to have been more secure in America than in England. Few colonists ever found things so bad as to resort to murder. Between 1663 and 1775 only twelve murders, five of them premeditated, were committed by white men in Connecticut. The famous English highwayman had no counterpart in America, and even the footpads of the cities, where crimes were more numerous and vicious, were pale imitations of British models. Organized vice was nowhere to be found, even in the most worldly seaports. The better economic conditions of the meaner sort had much to do with this noticeably lower level in the number and brutality of crimes.

The sex habits of the colonists, especially those of the Puritans, have received much attention from popular historians. Since there was no Dr. Kinsey to inquire and report, the total picture of sexual behavior is quite confused; an excellent case can be made for or against the virtue of the colonists, depending on the manner in which available statistics and contemporary judgments are handled. Certainly no one ever will determine finally whether bundling was an open invitation to lechery or the final test of the purity in Puritanism. It is reasonably safe to conclude that sex habits and morals were neither better nor worse than those of later times. Considering the coarseness of the age, the low character of many immigrants, and the lack of recreational outlets of a more wholesome character, one might even say that the record was excellent. The whole number of perversions and illicit acts recorded in ever-curious New England must be reckoned quite normal when spread over 150 years. What Bradford said of early Plymouth was probably true of most times and places in the colonies: "hear . . . is not more evills in this kind, nor nothing nere so many by proportion, as in other places; but they are hear more discovered and seen." Morbid publicity about sexual misconduct was to be expected in an age that had little else exciting to discuss, bemoan, or envy.

As to the level of public and private morality, the honest thing to say, much as it may pain the Daughters of This and Sons of That, is that our ancestors were not really any more virtuous or industrious or magnanimous than we are. They, too, got embroiled in political and social feuds—over land, currency, religion, representation, and matters of plain stubborn pride. They, too, railed against corruption, not because they had conquered it, but because they feared that it would conquer them. Gouging landlords, profiteering merchants, stingy school boards, grasping politicians, and apathetic voters were all common types in early America. So, too, were accomplished character assassins. The labels were different—"Papism" did the work of Communism and "filthy dalliance" of homosexuality—but the methods and motives were pretty much the same. Indeed, the more one reads old church records, court minutes, sermons, and newspapers, the more convinced he is that nothing ever really changes, at least nothing in the peculiar world of business and political ethics. Men in the colonies were honest and dishonest, open and sly, high-minded and sneaky, law-abiding and lawbreaking. If public morals were less corrupt than in England, this could be ascribed to the obvious truth that the stakes were not so high. The colonist demonstrated, in his blithe disregard of the Molasses Act of 1733, that he, like his descendants, would ignore any law contrary to the sense of the community. Smuggling and speakeasies are only two famous manifestations of the American refusal to obey "impossible" laws.

Many colonists were disturbed by evidence of lowered standards of public ethics. Letters bewailing civic corruption in the *New-York Gazette* of 1756 are hardly distinguishable from similar letters to the *New York Times* in 1956. Colonial Americans of a certain type, like modern Americans of the same type, thought the country was "going to hell in a bucket," and in no time at all. It should be mentioned in passing that the lottery, now regarded as corrupting and deplorable, was the favorite method of raising money in the colonies. Lotteries were conducted under both public and private auspices. They were extremely popular with all ranks and were used to raise funds for schools, colleges, charities, bridges, forts, and roads, as well as for churches of just about every denomination. They were rarely attacked on any grounds, never on grounds of being destructive of public virtue.

The modern historian, as he observes his colonial ancestors, is all but overcome by fumes of sack, brandy, beer, hard cider, port, punch, and "kill-devil" rum. The colonists had other outlets of recreation—hunting, fishing, horse racing, cockfighting, bowling, ball playing, boating, cards, and dancing—but the drinking of spirituous liquors swamped them all.

No important event was complete without heavy drinking, be it a wedding, funeral, baptism, house-raising, ship-launching, election, college commencement, or training day. No town or settlement was complete without one or more taverns. Contemporaneous accounts of eighteenth-century Boston listed one house in eight as a drinking place. And every household did its share of home brewing and distilling. One European visitor after another was amazed that even the "peasants" in America had fruit trees, not always realizing that apples and cher-

ries were for drinking rather than eating. Most
Americans seem to have spent their leisure hours
"tyed by the Lipps to a pewter engine," as Madam
Knight observed of the citizens of Dedham in 1704.
Drunkenness was probably the leading vice, or ave-
nue of release, in colonial America—all of which led a
gentleman in York County, Virginia, to declare in his
will:

> Having observed in the daies of my pilgrimage the de-
> bauches used at burialls tending much to the dishonour of
> God and his true religion, my will is that noe strong drinks
> be provided or spirits at my buriall.

Pulpit and press took repeated notice of the scan-
dalous amount of drinking at public functions and in
solitude, but there was no concerted move toward
prohibition or temperance in colonial times, whether
through public law or private co-operation. Cotton
Mather might deliver *A Serious Address to those
who unnecessarily Frequent the Tavern, and Often
spend the Evening in Publick Houses*, George Whitefield might preach of *The Heinous Sin of Drunkenness*, and Increase Mather might prophesy *Wo to
Drunkards*, but the tavern-frequenters and drunkards went right on drinking. Even these strong attacks were aimed at individual excesses rather than
root causes. Provincial legislation dealt with the
drinking problems of Indians, slaves, servants, and apprentices, not with those of the public at large.

The incidence of intoxication in colonial times is
of interest to the social historian for three reasons.
It shows once again the influence of English social
habits upon those of the colonists. It gives us some
idea of a way of life so rough and narrow that it
forced men into violent methods of forgetting their
troubles. And its unchallenged sway illustrates the
lack of a crusading spirit in the social attitudes of the
first Americans.

Colonial methods in dealing with unfortunate members of society were thoroughly in keeping with the English inheritance and pioneering environment. Little time, thought, or money was or could be devoted to care and protection of the poor and insane. Such people were looked upon as social nuisances rather than sociological problems, and methods of handling them were rough and often heartless.

Although many travelers and diarists agreed with Andrew Burnaby—"America is formed for happiness. . . . In a course of 1,200 miles I did not see a single object that solicited charity"—the records of town and parish reveal that the poor were also with us in the colonies. Their peculiar problem was handled in a number of ways, all of them crude. New England towns relied heavily on the harsh technique of "warning-out." Several cities built almshouses and then showed what they thought of the "honest poor" by also housing criminals in them. All colonies subscribed as best they could to the principles of the Elizabethan Poor Laws of 1601, which placed responsibility on local authorities—"every towne providing for their owne poore." Funds were raised through the property tax, and the poor who could not be dispatched or set to labor in workhouses were cared for by families under agreement with town or parish. Poor children were usually bound out as apprentices. Cities and larger settlements turned increasingly to institutional care and to a differentiation between paupers and "sturdy beggars," but early Americans never could rid themselves of the notion that poverty was somehow criminal, that it was wrong to fight against what Franklin called "the order of God and Nature, which perhaps has appointed want and misery as the proper punishments for, and cautions against, as well as necessary consequences of, idleness and extravagance."

The accepted methods of treating the insane were

punishment, repression, and indifference. Ignorance, superstition, lack of public funds, and tradition helped maintain an attitude of cruelty and carelessness toward the feebleminded. The Pennsylvania Hospital, founded in 1751, was the first in America to give the insane any sort of institutional treatment; not until 1773 did a colony (Virginia) erect a separate establishment to house and care for them. The New England way was for the most part the American way: take them into private homes or drive them out of town. This entry of November 10, 1742, in the Boston records saves me pages of commentary on colonial methods of handling social problems:

Complaint being made by Mr. Cooke that Mr. Samuel Coolidge formerly chaplain of the Castle, is now in this Town & in a Distracted Condition & very likely to be a Town Charge.

Voted, That Mr. Savell Warn him out of Town according to law.

The punishment of crime and immorality was, of course, severe and callous. Imprisonment, except of debtors and persons awaiting trial, was virtually unknown. Convicted men paid their debt to society in one installment—by execution, fine, exposure to ridicule or shame, mutilation, or corporal punishment. Penology was a social science unknown to the colonies. English traditions and frontier conditions rendered the responsible authorities wholly devoid of concern over the rehabilitation of the criminal or of interest in how he became one in the first place. Yet here, too, the trend was toward more humanitarian methods. The death penalty was progressively restricted to only the most serious crimes, such as piracy, murder, and arson. Branding and mutilation, if not whipping, were inflicted less and less frequently. Criminal codes remained severe but were less vindictively enforced. Pennsylvania offers the most interesting case study for the social historian. An original code of unusual mildness was made considerably more severe in the early eighteenth century, so severe indeed as to call forth vetoes from the Privy Council; yet the cruel and unusual penalties seem to have been designed to frighten rather than punish. It was, however, totally characteristic of the age for government to react to an increase in crime by stiffening old penalties and devising new ones.

I have already had cause to examine Negro slavery in the colonies and have pointed out that indifference toward the plight of the slave and presumption of his permanent inferiority were the common attitudes of the white man. It need only be added that attacks on slavery on humanitarian grounds and organized movements to free, protect, or educate the Negro were few and feeble before 1765. The protests of John Woolman, Anthony Benezet, Elias Neau, Samuel Sewall, George Keith, John Hepburn, the Germantown Mennonites of 1688, the missionaries of the Society for the Propagation of the Gospel, and the Society of Friends were saintly voices in a callous wilderness.

This review of colonial attitudes toward women and children, crime and punishment, the use and abuse of liquor, and the care of the unfortunate is evidence that the level of social feeling was low yet steadily rising. It was low in the colonies principally because it was low in the countries from which the colonists had come, because they, too, were children of a world that was crude, callous, ignorant, and indifferent in matters that concerned man's relations with man. It was rising for the very same reason, because all over the Atlantic world prophetic voices were being raised ever louder in protest against brutality and apathy. Some of these voices spoke from England to America, some from America to

England and the rest of the Western world. All fore-told a day when organized humanitarianism would bring law and social action to the support of a new sense of compassion and concern for troubled man.

I hope that I have not smashed any legitimate idols in the course of this review of colonial habits and morals, for such, surely, was not my intention. Our colonial fathers were indeed an astonishing breed. The breed, however, was astonishingly human, combining in its total pattern of behavior the virtues and vices, strengths and weaknesses, delights and despairs of all mankind. They were not all saints; we are not all sinners. America has not moved steadily downhill in morals and manners from some wonderful Paradise Lost.

IV

Developments in colonial society worked both for and against liberty, self-government, and political equality. So vital an institution as the militia was in some times and places a leveling, democratizing influence, in others a breeder of class distinctions. So widespread a social outlook as that of the middle class, in which a disingenuous mania for rank vied with an invigorating spirit of independence, was likewise a mixed blessing. Yet for the most part these developments were creating an environment in which free government and democratic ideas could prosper. Four broad social developments were especially influential in the rise of liberty: the firm establishment of a middle class; the emergence of a native aristocracy; the increasingly fluid character of the social structure; and the periodic eruption of social grievances into class and sectional conflict.

American democracy has always been middle-class democracy, a celebrated scheme of society and government from which aristocracy and proletariat, to the extent that each has existed, have alike been excluded from full reception and participation. Since our own bourgeoisie has been a large one, counting (according to various modern estimates) up to 80 or 90 per cent of the population, American identification of democracy with the political rule and social habits of the middle class has not been so fraudulent as many foreign observers would have us believe. In any case, free government in the United States has been a reasonably faithful reflection of the virtues and faults of the middle class. The rise of this class in the colonial era and its struggle for the stakes of political and economic power were one of the great determinants of early American history.

The rise of the middle class was neither so steady nor so massive as might easily have been the case. At least one healthy society of self-respecting yeomen, that of seventeenth-century Virginia, was sapped by conditions peculiar to the tobacco colonies. In another province, New York, a neo-feudal land system based on greed and corruption obstructed the natural process that had taken place in early Virginia. Yet even in these colonies the middling sort could not be wiped out, and in Pennsylvania ("the heaven of the farmers, the paradise of the mechanics"), New Jersey, New England, and the western counties of the South the yeoman became so common a species as to share heavily in government and set the tone of society. Among the forces that sustained the advance of the middling sort were the importance of this class and its principles in England, the middle-class background of many thousands of immigrants, the infinity of opportunities open to the industrious and frugal, and the long rise, despite temporary setbacks, of the productive capacity of the colonies and of the prices paid by the world for their staples and wares. The very conditions that helped create a class structure were at the same time hastening the triumph of the one class whose virtues and attitudes could vitiate most of the evil effects of stratification.

These virtues and attitudes were for the most part welcome supports to liberty and self-government. If the average farmer or shopkeeper had too much respect for the gentry, too little compassion for the meaner sort, and too lively a concern for the symbols and privileges of his own substratum in the middling band, these attitudes, especially the first two, were a good deal less pronounced than those of the middle class in England. And on the credit side of the ledger, the middle class could count several imposing contributions to ordered liberty.

First, the middling sort provided the chief stabilizing influence in religion, politics, economic affairs, and human relations. No people, however virtuous and politically talented, can make a success of free government unless it rests on a broad floor of social and economic stability. The small farmers, independent artisans, and shopkeepers of the American colonies—most of them men who were sensible in religion, diligent in business, steady in politics, and law-abiding in social attitude—gave a measure of strength to society that neither the fancies of the aristocracy nor the abasement of the lower class could shake. If thousands went off after Whitefield like men slapping bees, tens of thousands stood fast in the ancient ways. A certain measure of conservatism is necessary to the proper functioning of free society, and the healthy conservatism of the eighteenth century was largely a middle-class product.

The middle-class point of view became the dominant feature of the colonial mind. Industry, frugality, honesty, and self-reliance were celebrated not only for the rewards they brought yeoman and artisan, but also for the support they gave free government and progressive society. The colonial middle class first gave expression to the peculiar mixture of individualism and co-operation that has characterized the American psychology through most of our history. The political influence of the virtues and beliefs of the middling sort was personified in the life and accomplishments of their great expounder, Benjamin Franklin.

Finally, the middle class was both product and crucible of the process of "leveling" to which so many foreign observers bore friendly or unfriendly witness. An English officer said of the New Englanders in 1759, "They came out with a levelling spirit, and they retain it." Lord Adam Gordon, observing the same section in 1765, spoke of "that ancient rugged Spirit of Levelling, early Imported from home, and successfully nursed, and cherished." As to Boston, "The levelling principle here, every where Operates strongly, and takes the lead, every body has property, and every body knows it." A writer in the *Pennsylvania Journal* in 1756 declared:

The People of this Province are generally of the middling Sort, and at present pretty much upon a Level. They are chiefly industrious Farmers, Artificers or Men in Trade; they enjoy and are fond of Freedom, and *the meanest among them* thinks he has a right to Civility from the greatest.

The better sort might moan that politics was fast becoming the province of "mechanicks and ignorant wretches, obstinate to the last degree," but the average man of the middling sort felt himself neither ignorant nor wretched. The meaner sort might lament their degraded and voteless station, but the average man believed that no wall but their own laziness barred them from the broad plateau of middling equality he occupied so proudly. The drive toward social equality, which was to come to fruition in the Jacksonian era, was well under way in the colonial period. It was the middling not the meaner sort that launched this drive.

The self-creation of an indigenous aristocracy was a mixed blessing for the cause of liberty and self-government in the colonies. The acquisition of wealth and pretensions by a small group of hard-driving commercial capitalists made the existence and labors of the meaner sort a social necessity. As the upper class pulled itself up, the lower classes were forced lower. The result was a class structure in which the gaps between classes were a constant threat to social solidarity. And since in most societies, especially young ones, political power flows toward the centers of social and economic power, the new American aristocracy became in time a tight-fisted, even oligarchic ruling class in almost every colony. In the end, however, because of circumstances over which it had little control, the aristocracy was to go along with and even lead the procession moving fitfully toward self-government. Even the most democratically oriented historians consider this class to have been an essential ingredient of early American liberty.

A clear recognition of the origins, pursuits, and political attitudes of the colonial gentry will help toward an understanding of its sometimes voluntary, more often involuntary, contributions to this liberty. Few of the leading families in Boston, New York, Philadelphia, or even Virginia could lay claim to gentle ancestry. Cadwallader Colden of New York was only exaggerating for the sake of emphasis when he wrote in 1765 that "the most opulent families, in our own memory, have arisen from the lowest rank of the people." Indeed, it can be argued that the better sort in the colonies were a self-seeking plutocracy rather than a duty-conscious aristocracy. The records speak of an upper class, whether situated in Salem or Prince George County, that was more consistently devoted to business management and capital investment than to culture, sports, and the other pursuits of refined leisure. The first American aristocracy was a working aristocracy. The planter hunted profits more often than foxes; the merchant drove bargains more often than blooded horses. For few American gentlemen, no matter how many generations removed from the founder of their fortunes, was leisure an end in itself.

The one thing that saved the better sort from the harsh label of plutocracy was their devotion to political affairs and public service. The colonial gentleman did not flee from political activity; he sought office avidly and held it tenaciously, because of the prestige and profits attached to it, and because of the inherited belief that public service was a duty of the gentry. Governor's council, assembly, provincial judiciary, county court, vestry, and often even the machinery of town government were largely in the hands of the upper class. The way in which the aristocrat made his contributions to the rise of liberty is testimony to the great truth that democracy is the work of all manner of men, not just of goodhearted democrats.

The office-holding aristocracy took the lead in the struggle between provincial assembly and royal governor. If some members of the ruling class rallied around the governor and supported his attempts to apply prerogative to a stiff-necked people, many more championed the designing measures that sought to exalt the assembly as the guardian of colonial rights and profits. It is a question open to debate whether the gentlemen of tidewater Virginia were more anxious to make the House of Burgesses a genuine legislature at the expense of the royal prerogative, or to keep it their own instrument at the expense of the underrepresented western counties. In any case, the protesting assemblies of 1765, the key instruments of self-government and schools of political thought, had been largely shaped and were now largely manned by men who considered themselves

the better sort. No assembly made a more resolute
protest against the Stamp Act than that of South
Carolina; yet eligibility for this body that spoke of
"the freedom of a people" was limited to men with
five hundred acres of land, ten slaves, or property
valued at £1,000!

At the same time that colonial aristocrats were
bringing new vitality to old institutions of self-government, they were helping to popularize a liberal
political philosophy. Although the country party in
the assembly struggled chiefly to improve its own
position in a high-level war with the governor and his
party, it had to believe, for the sake of its own morale, that it fought for the whole province against
executive encroachment. And since it needed the
support of the middle class and even of the lower
classes, its arguments were couched in the language
of Pym, Hampden, Sidney, and Locke. The lower orders of men, who were supposed to sit by quietly and
await the outcome of this internecine political strife,
could hardly be blamed for coming to believe some of
the things they read and heard about the rights of
Englishmen and the common weal.

The workings of this strange process of education
in liberal political thought were especially apparent
in New York, where Livingstons assaulted De Lanceys
in the provincial press as if they themselves were
apostles of pure liberty and their opponents agents
of blackest oppression. Zenger's *New-York Weekly
Journal* and the short-lived *Independent Reflector*,
two of the most radical journals in colonial America,
were simply journalistic outposts of the country
wing of the New York aristocracy. If these aristocrats were a "dilettante democracy . . . equally
anxious to clip the pinions of ambitious royalty and'
to curb the insolence of the unfettered mob," they
nevertheless chose to battle the agents of royalty
with phrases that had a special appeal to the "mob."

The pre-1765 popularity of radical Whig doctrines in New York was largely the work of men who were aristocrats to the core, the eminent triumvirate of William Livingston, William Smith, Jr., and John Morin Scott. Here as elsewhere the lasting results of the assembly's campaign against the governors were the strengthening of elective institutions and popularizing of progressive principles.

We must be careful not to hold in ridicule the colonial aristocrat's devotion to liberty and justice, however much he might have defined these words to his own advantage. Certainly among the planting aristocracy of the South the spirit of liberty was vigorous and sincere. Real or imagined attempts by the Crown to restrict the processes of self-government evoked some of the most "leveling" and "republican" protests of the colonial period—not from the democratic Cohees but from the aristocratic Tuckahoes. Said Burke of the Southern colonies:

There is, however, a circumstance attending these colonies, which . . . makes the spirit of liberty still more high and haughty than in those to the northward. It is, that in Virginia and the Carolinas they have a vast multitude of slaves. Where this is the case in any part of the world, those who are free, are by far the most proud and jealous of their freedom. Freedom is to them not only an enjoyment, but a kind of rank and privilege.

A keen observer on the spot, Andrew Burnaby, had already voiced similar observations:

The public or political character of the Virginians, corresponds with their private one: they are haughty and jealous of their liberties, impatient of restraint, and can scarcely bear the thought of being controuled by any superior power.

While both these Englishmen were speaking of the planters of the South, their remarks could be extended to the aristocracy everywhere. For men like the New York triumvirate "liberty" was something more than a helpful word with which to bolster arguments against the royal prerogative.

Finally, we cannot forget the memorable part played by the pro-American wing of the aristocracy in the period between the Stamp Act and the Declaration of Independence. It was to this class of men— the only class with a common outlook and with acquaintances that bridged the gaps of intercolonial rivalry, mistrust, and ignorance—that the mass of Americans turned for leadership in this decade. Mere mention of the names of Washington, Jefferson, Lee, Mason, Carroll, Rutledge, Pinckney, Otis, Hancock, Trumbull, Ellery, Morris, Livingston, Dickinson, and Schuyler should be enough to remind us of the role of the landed and merchant aristocracy in the Revolution. James Logan had written of the New England colonies in 1732 that "while there are no noble or Great and Ancient Families . . . they cannot Rebel." If an authentic aristocracy was a prerequisite to self-government in the colonies, then by 1765 this prerequisite was in being. The colonies could not possibly have resisted or revolted without these men and their unique training in the school of political leadership.

V

Another broad development that favored the growth of political liberty was an increase in fluidity throughout the social structure. Slowly but massively the colonies were beginning to move toward that bumptious spirit and condition of equality that was to characterize the American social order in the first half of the nineteenth century and to eliminate property as a prerequisite of political activity. Like most other major sociological trends in American history, the loosening-up of colonial society had bad effects as well as good. Yet it seems clear in retrospect that it was both confirmation and cause of the long-range movement toward political democracy.

We have already noted one instance of this increasing fluidity: the fact that classes in the colonies, however well defined and accepted, were in no sense closed corporations denying admittance to those born in other classes. Passage from one class to another grew progressively more possible throughout the eighteenth century, except perhaps in semifeudal Virginia and South Carolina. In the cities, where fortunes could be more easily won or lost, the social ladder seemed as much a challenge as an obstruction to the ambitious tradesman. Since wealth was the chief criterion of social status, the general increase in economic opportunity in the eighteenth century was matched by an increase in social mobility. Observant Americans were well aware of this development. Said a writer to a Philadelphia newspaper in 1776:

> Is not one half of the property in the city of Philadelphia owned by men who wear LEATHER APRONS?
> Does not the other half belong to men whose fathers or grandfathers wore LEATHER APRONS?

The wonder is that he did not add something about "leather aprons to leather aprons in three generations."

Another sign of a society growing less rigid was the change in attitudes among the different classes. In particular, the lower-class attitude of deference and upper-class attitude of condescension were slowly being converted into a more healthy relationship, one of respect that worked both ways on the social scale. This, of course, was a more selective attitude, in which the person, not his station, was the primary determinant. Contempt rather than respect continued to mark the feelings of the better sort about "rioting sailors and mechanicks"; bitter hatred rather than respect often marked those of the meaner sort about the class that often left them no outlet but rioting. The middle class remained steadfast in its familiar attitude of friendly mistrust toward the class above and the class below.

Still another sign of increased fluidity—many would have called it a sign of disintegration—was the improved status of women, children, and dependents everywhere, and of servants in the North. Women became less subordinate, children less exposed to discipline, dependents less put upon, and servants less subject to the master's whims. This, of course, is a very general observation, for the shift toward more tenderness and trust was at best one of emphasis. Yet the evidence of diaries and letters points unmistakably to a freer and more pleasant pattern of social intercourse within the family and out of doors. This trend was matched, as we have already seen, by a rise in concern over social problems and in compassion for the unfortunate.

The New England towns, of which there were more than 550 in 1776, are ideal laboratories in which to observe the trend toward a more open, undisciplined, flexible society. Frontier and city were environments in which mobility was part of the natural order of things, but the changes that took place during the eighteenth century in the monolithic structure of the older towns reveal the sweep of this trend. The New England towns were unable to withstand the combined impact of the expansion of population, secularization of life, and growth of commerce that molded all social developments in eighteenth-century America. The growth of interest in the world outside, the sharpening of class antagonisms, the decline of clerical leadership, the emigration of offshoots of the best old stock, the easier influx of "strangers," the increasing frivolity of training day, the appearance of new and other-minded churches, the proliferation of household manufactures, the unflagging popularity of the tavern, the upswing in sexual immorality—not all these were welcome developments; indeed, some were most unfortunate. Yet they indicate relaxation of the rigid communalism that all towns had aspired to and many had achieved.

The changes in old towns were reflected in looser methods of settling new ones. Grants were now made to individuals rather than to congregations, and the resulting patterns of settlement were dispersed rather than communal. The New England town did not disintegrate under the pressures of the eighteenth century. It was far too tough and functional a social organism to collapse that easily. Yet it did undergo an extensive modification that can best be described as the rise of self-centered as opposed to community-minded individualism. Much that was good sank slowly into discard, but so, too, did much that was outmoded and intolerant. The residuum of unity that persisted was relatively unforced, rising from the plain man at the bottom rather than imposed by the gentleman at the top.

American society in the eighteenth century continued to exhibit three prominent features that had appeared in the seventeenth to distinguish it from England and Europe: first, there were relatively fewer people in both the upper and lower classes—always excepting, in the latter instance, the Negro slaves; second, passage from one class to the next, and especially from both directions into the middle class, was easier; and third, the colonies were well on the way to achieving a revolutionary compromise between the new demands of the individual for a life of his own and the old demands of the group for social unity. Unfriendly visitors and officials could sneer as they pleased about "leveling," but most Americans agreed with the greatest American, "I see no

Country of Europe where there is so much general
Comfort & Happiness as in America."

Controversy is the life thrust of the open society.
The groups that develop within such a society must
inevitably come into conflict over the stakes of social, economic, and political power. Particularly in an
active and growing community will parties, economic interests, churches, sections, and classes squabble among themselves for preferment. The mature
society is one that has recognized this condition by
creating institutions that foster the spirit of compromise and techniques that make possible the
peaceful resolution of serious differences. Colonial
America, an active and growing community, had its
full share of controversy, especially of a class or sectional character. We have already noted the contest-
ing classes. The basic sectional cleavage was between
the settled seaboard and pioneering back country.
Since the former was the realm of the aristocracy
and the latter the haven of the small farmer,
sectional and class conflict often went hand in hand.

The seventeenth century set the style for the
eighteenth. From the first settlement in each colony, groups and sections argued bitterly over land,
economic policy, religion, and political power. At
times antagonisms erupted into riots that exposed
deep cleavages in society; and once, on the occasion
of Bacon's Rebellion in Virginia in 1676, the scourge
of civil war was visited upon the land. Other instances of class and sectional hostility in the seventeenth century were the anti-proprietary revolts in
Maryland (1652-1689), similar outbreaks in South
Carolina (1685-1691) and North Carolina (1677-
1679), the long struggle between aristocratic and
popular forces in New York that came to a climax
in Leisler's Revolt (1689-1691), and a volley of spats
over land and government in New Jersey. Most par-
ticipants in these large and small revolts were Eng-

lishmen or the sons of Englishmen, trustees of a tradition of law and order. Their outbursts of violence, most of which were motivated by antagonisms within a colony rather than between colony and home authorities, were therefore especially convincing proof of the growing complexity of American society.

Six bones of contention fed the controversies of the eighteenth century: land, currency, religion, representation, government activity, and simple class antagonism. In most instances, grievances in three or four of these categories worked together to incite an oppressed class or section to protest and an oppressing class or section to reprisal. And generally there was something to be said for each side in the dispute.

I have already called attention in Chapter II, to the unfortunate circumstance underlying most conflicts over land in the colonial period: the fact that it was the one thing for which the common man longed and the most rewarding type of capital investment. The result was a perpetual, protean struggle between settler and speculator, the one seeking productive and unencumbered land at the cheapest possible price, the other seeking the largest possible return on his risk capital. Quit rents, conflicting titles, squatting, timber cutting, land engrossing, and tenantry only added to a confusion of rights and purposes out of which social conflicts grew naturally. In Pennsylvania, Virginia, the Carolinas, western New England, New York, and above all New Jersey, disputes flourished between settlers and proprietors, debtors and collectors, farmers and speculators, squatters and landlords, and between settlers armed with conflicting titles. Courts, assembly, council, and units of local government were all cockpits of contention over disputed titles and claims; and when the men with the soundest claim, those who actually worked the land, could get no satisfaction from petition and litigation, they resorted to rump meetings, riot, and armed resistance. Class conflict over the land reached its bitter peak in New Jersey. The attempt of the proprietors of East Jersey to assert their legal rights was met head-on by the determination of the settlers to resist all oppressive rents and claims. The result was a decade (1745-1755) of rioting, squatting, political anarchy, legal and political maneuvering, and appeal to "the Rules of natural Justice." Eventually almost the entire northern part of the colony was in an uproar against the landlords; the uproar did not, however, prevent the steady rise of economic prosperity!

The demand for easy money has divided Americans for more than 250 years. Not a single colony in the eighteenth century could escape the tensions that lead to and derive from the issuance of paper money. The conflict between the agrarian debtor of the middle class and the mercantile creditor of the upper class was bitter, for it was essentially a struggle over the price the latter should pay the former for the fruits of his labor. For the most part, the forces that favored either a contracted or expanded currency carried on their vendetta in legislature and press. The Crown, which had a monetary policy harder than any that was popular in the colonies, intervened repeatedly to demolish the schemes of debt-ridden farmers and their allies among the lesser merchants. Occasionally, however, these differences in opinion over the necessity and effects of promissory notes, bills of credit, and land banks threatened to erupt into violence. During the memorable land bank controversy in Massachusetts in 1741, the struggle between the farmers, who controlled the assembly, and the merchants, who rallied around the governor, came near to tearing the province apart. Only the determined action of Governor Belcher and his supporters prevented a riotous march of the farmers on Boston; and only a naked display of imperial power, an act of Parliament extending the Bubble Act of 1720 to the colonies, forced the inflationist party to abandon the land bank. The outlawing of the land bank left a heritage of radical agrarian antipathy toward the merchants of Boston that was of huge consequence for the future course of Massachusetts politics. In Rhode Island, to the contrary, the merchants took the most severe beating, since they were constantly forced to accept payment of country debts in paper currency "Esteemed upon the worst footing of any in North America." Only another act of Parliament (in 1751) could halt the riotous inflation resulting from the creation of nine land banks in forty years. By this and subsequent acts Parliament effectively outlawed all but the most sober issues of paper currency in New England and the other colonies. This did nothing to relieve the tension between debtor and creditor in America.

There is little that need be added to the discussion in Chapter III of the class and sectional antagonisms aroused by the Great Awakening. As was said in that context, the upsurge in religious feeling was generally primitive in character, appealing primarily to the poor and despised, revolting the well-born, well-educated, and well-to-do. The splitting of Congregational, Reformed, and Presbyterian churches into camps that conformed generally to class lines was a staggering blow to many a hitherto peaceful village society. The excesses of enthusiasm caused even liberal spirits like Jonathan Mayhew to speak in acid language of "the meaner sort," and conservatives, convinced that the whole social order was in danger, adopted attitudes toward the "giddy, ignorant people" that were crude and contemptuous. The enthusiasts, on the other hand, did as much to quicken the spirit of social equality as to revive the spirit of true religion.

A fourth grievance that did much to stir up social controversy was the problem of representation in the assemblies. In many colonies the western counties, largely inhabited by small farmers, were kept deliberately underrepresented by the old counties, largely controlled by conservative merchants or landholders. In 1760 Lancaster County in Pennsylvania was nearly twice as heavily populated as Bucks County, yet it sent only four representatives to the assembly against eight from the older area. Discrimination against newly settled areas was even more flagrant in Virginia and the Carolinas. The persistent petitions of frontier counties for more equitable representation and the persistent refusal of tidewater counties to pay heed added fuel to the fires of bitterness between sections and classes.

Still another bone of contention was the refusal of the ruling class in several colonies to adjust or operate the machinery of government in favor of the newer sections. One example was eastern hostility to schemes to raise farm prices and scale down debts. Another was the lukewarm attitude of settled counties toward frontier demands for protection against Indian warfare. The infamous riot of the "Paxton Boys" in 1764 was the bitter fruit of this kind of contention in Pennsylvania. A third instance was the intolerable difficulty, travel, and expense involved in going to law in the newer counties. In many of these counties sheriffs, judges, and lawyers were simply agents of the eastern ruling class whom small farmers denounced as "cursed hungry Caterpillars, that will eat out the very Bowels of our Commonwealth, if they are not pulled down from their Nests in a very short time." Many sober, hardworking pioneers were convinced that the provincial government was working against rather than for their protection and welfare.

Not all class antagonisms were sectional in nature.

Classes could also exist side by side with little respect or affection for one another. This was especially true in the developing cities, where wealth had accumulated in amounts grand enough to permit many aristocratic families to engage in ostentatious display. The widening economic gulf between the gentry and the meaner sort had a disruptive effect on class relations. There is a great deal of evidence of simple antagonism between rich and poor in New York, Charleston, and Philadelphia; and even in supposedly stable Boston, poor rioted in resentment of rich and rich despised poor.

The basic sectional division during this period was between west and east within each colony rather than between one group of colonies and another. The west—such counties as Lancaster, York, and Cumberland in Pennsylvania, Frederick in Maryland, Augusta in Virginia, Orange and Anson in North Carolina, and Orangeburg and Ninety-Six Precincts in South Carolina—was the area of protest; the east was the area of indifference and reaction. Mixed in national origin (with the Scotch-Irish giving the mixture its special flavor), dissenting in religion, democratic in politics, and leveling in social attitudes, the men of the "Old West" felt entitled to a better deal in representation, religious freedom, prices, taxation, debts, protection, and the administration of justice. In many a colony in 1764 civil war seemed more likely than war with Britain. Only once, however, did the grievances of the back country explode into sustained and organized violence—the famous Regulator movement in North Carolina (1768-1771), an uprising of yeomen settlers against the office-holding, privileged class and its agents. An inequitable tax system, corrupt and oppressive officials, callous land engrossing, excessive judicial fees, and underrepresentation were the wrongs that touched off this display of mob violence. The Regulators interfered bodily with the operation of courts, raided jails to release imprisoned fellows, resisted evictions and collections, and launched attacks on homes and offices of hated county officials. The showdown took place at Alamance in May, 1771, when Governor Tryon's militia, topheavy with officers from the planter class, routed the Regulator army of some two thousand men. This show of force and the execution of seven ringleaders brought the movement to collapse. Hundreds of Regulators moved on to the west; the others submitted and were granted amnesty. But hate between east and west was now part of life in North Carolina —as it was in several other colonies to the north and south. Alamance was not the first battle of the Revolution but the last and largest sectional uprising of the colonial period.

The importance of class and sectional controversy for the rise of political liberty should be obvious to even the most casual student of the colonial period. Group antagonism was a sign of a growing society, a cause of major readjustments within it, and a spur to political participation. An English observer remarked in 1760 that "a spirit of party is universally prevalent in America." He might have remarked more accurately that the colonists seemed to be coming to life politically. And he might have noted, too, that as the men of the west and lower classes came to think and talk politically, they were only too pleased to borrow from eastern aristocrats the language of Whiggery and natural rights.

There is little to add in conclusion to this description of colonial society. The significant features of that society are manifest: It was stratified, simple, callous, and communal; it was also becoming more fluid, complex, humane, and individualistic. Most important, it was plastic and self-directing. The colonists were restricted by imperial design and inherited traditions, yet the design was shadowy and the traditions quite malleable when detached from their institutional supports in England.

Despite instructions and influences that flowed from home, the colonists were able to build a society that answered their own needs and understandings. The early years in Georgia are proof of this truth. The Trustees wanted small landholdings in tail male, free labor, a prohibition on rum, and paternal government; the settlers wanted large landholdings in fee simple, slavery, rum, and an assembly. It took a few years, but the settlers got what they wanted, even if much that they wanted was bad. Slavery and land grabbing would not be the last grave social mistakes Americans would commit. The path to social democracy would prove rocky and unending, but at least it would be one of their own making.

VI

The Golden Age Succeeds the Iron: The Colonial Mind

———————◆◆◆◆◆———————

The rise of liberty in colonial America owed much to the unfolding of intellectual and cultural forces. The spirit of liberty—whether political, social, religious, or economic—was more deeply imbedded in the colonial mind than in colonial institutions, and it would seem proper to close this survey of early American life by discovering what this mind believed, what it inherited or imported from England and Europe, what it learned in the wilderness, how it was trained, and through what agencies it expressed and improved itself.

It may be misleading to speak of "the colonial mind." Although there was an ultimate unity to intellectual life, it was probably no more important, and was in many ways less striking, than the sharp contrasts in thought and culture that arose out of diversities of time, section, proximity to sea or frontier, religion, national origin, occupation, and class. Yet this term may serve as convenient label for these aspects of colonial life: education, science, literature, the arts, philosophy, and political thought. Before I proceed to examine each of these slices of the colonial mind, let me set down several capital facts about thought and culture in colonial America.

I

For all its importance in our scheme of historical values, the colonial mind can lay only a tiny claim to serious consideration in the intellectual history of Western man. The general level of literary and artistic achievement or comprehension was low; and, except for Jonathan Edwards and Benjamin Franklin, the colonies did not produce a single intellect worthy of universal contemplation. Many colonists were aware of their shortcomings and hopeful of correcting them. Their oft-expressed sense of inferiority had the ring of challenge rather than despair. Americans looked forward confidently to the rise of an indigenous culture. "After the first Cares for the Necessaries of Life are over," Franklin wrote, "we shall come to think of the Embellishments. Already some of our young Geniuses begin to lisp Attempts at Painting, Poetry and Musick."

The starkness of early American culture was primarily a result of the colonists' struggles with the wilderness. "How can he get wisdom that holdeth the plow and that glorieth in the goad, that driveth oxen, and is occupied in their labors and whose talk is of bullocks?" asked Governor Lewis Morris of the New Jersey Assembly in 1745. "How indeed?" the assembled plowmen might have asked in rebuttal. We shall never know how many Newtons and Lockes, or at least Hoadlys and Addisons, might have arisen even in New Jersey had there been less need to talk of bullocks and more chance to talk of buskins. When we consider the work that had to be done in America simply to prepare the ground for the growth of culture, especially to amass the surplus of wealth that makes it possible for society to support poets and artists, we may well conclude that the level of culture and incidence of genius were both remarkably high.

As one hopeful gentleman wrote to James Franklin's *Rhode Island Gazette:*

In the Rise of States, the Arts of War and Peace, Agriculture, and the like, are of necessity more attended to than Erudition and Politeness, that comes on of course afterwards, when the *Golden Age* succeeds the *Iron.* So that instead of wondering why our Country has produced so few good Writers, and why those which have been produced, have not always given a general *Satisfaction,* we may rather admire at the contrary.

Education, science, theology, philosophy, literature, journalism, manners, art, architecture, and political thought were largely English in origin and expression. Whether the process of transfer was largely unconscious, as in the seventeenth century when most colonials were transplanted Englishmen, or largely conscious, as in the eighteenth when fifth-generation Americans of the upper and upper-middle classes still looked eastward for inspiration, the influence of English thought and culture was commanding. The processes of inheritance and importation were, to be sure, selective. The colonists absorbed those elements of English culture they found rational and serviceable; they rejected many that appeared outworn or corrupting or ill-adapted to the wilderness. Yet as one reads colonial newspapers, studies the curriculum of the colleges, browses in the libraries of Cotton Mather and Robert Carter, and hears in his imagination the debates of the assemblies, he must admit that the adjective "English-American" rather than "American" describes the dominant culture, even as late as 1765.

The colonial mind was thoroughly Christian in its approach to education, philosophy, and social thought. At the same time, it was constantly in evolution, and the most interesting development was the secularization of thought, aspirations, and culture.

This process, which was quickened by the advance of individualism, rationalism, skepticism, and humanism, can be traced in almost every province of intellectual life: in education, literature, art, science, philosophy, political and social thought, and even in religion itself. The Christian religion grew less influential as the colonies moved toward maturity and liberty. Yet this decline in influence was only relative; the variants of Christianity remained a major determinant of the culture of every class and section.

A third great force, the idea of human liberty, worked with Christianity and the English heritage to bring an ultimate unity to the deep-seated intellectual and cultural diversities in early America. Liberty, in one guise or another, was the aspiration of most men and the characteristic of most currents of thought that moved westward to America. The total environment was one in which prophets of freedom, exponents of a rising humanism, could preach with maximum efficiency, and in which prophets of perdition, defenders of a dying obscurantism, could delay but not prevent the coming of a new order. Liberating systems of thought and culture—Whiggery, rationalism, the new science—were welcomed with acclaim, especially in the eighteenth century. Harsh systems like Puritanism grew steadily more humane. The individualistic, rationalistic, and popular elements in this great way of life seemed to thrive in American soil, while the authoritarian, dogmatic, and aristocratic elements bore withered fruit. The American mind of 1765 still harbored elements of dogma and despair, but it had absorbed many more of reason and optimism. The most powerful single force for freedom in early America was the devotion to liberty in the colonial mind.

II

The first subject of concern in an assessment of the colonial mind must be the character, purposes, instruments, and achievements of the system of education. Although the total picture of this phase of colonial life, as of so many others, is one of confusion compounded by lack of reliable statistics and observations, the outlines are sufficiently distinct to permit a number of generalizations.

Two attributes of colonial education are especially alien and therefore intriguing to the modern mind: the manner in which it conformed to the demands of the class structure, and the extent to which it was motivated and directed by institutionalized religion. Class and religion are still important forces in certain phases of American education, but they are by no means as important as two centuries ago. I have already noted, in Chapter V, the significance of the class structure in colonial America; it should come as no surprise to learn that the pattern of education conformed to assumptions of social inequality. The character and duration of a child's education were determined by the status of his parents. Most children were cut off completely by custom and economic necessity from secondary and higher education. And most men who gave any thought to the subject agreed with William Smith of Philadelphia that each social group—the "gentlemen," those "design'd for the Mechanic Professions," and "all the remaining People of the Country"—should receive a different type of education. Neither the fact nor the ideal of educational democracy had any standing in early America.

Religion and education were closely associated in the colonial mind. Although education, even in early Massachusetts, attempted to teach many things—

knowledge of the world, "good literature," virtue, manners, civic consciousness, business and professional skills—its chief purpose was to support revealed religion. Most institutions of education were begun and maintained by religious groups for religious ends. The Puritan ministers of New England and the Anglican missionaries of the Society for the Propagation of the Gospel are the best-remembered educators of the colonial era. The secularization of social aims in the eighteenth century did much to weaken the dominance of religion. New currents from abroad and new challenges of the environment turned men's thoughts to the secular, public, and utilitarian aspects of education. Yet religion, thanks in part to the tenacity of inherited assumptions about class structure and education, remained the central consideration. Even men so fundamentally skeptical as Colden and Franklin considered the Christian ethic the common element of education for every class and the marrow of education for the poor. More than this, they agreed with most other men of the period that education had a higher, more social purpose than the improvement or salvation of the individual. Indoctrination, the active inculcation of values—whether designed to reinforce true religion or "to form the Minds of the Youth, to Virtue, and to make them useful Members of the Society"—was the distinguishing mark of educational method in early America.

Education was largely a result of private solicitude and enterprise. Too much has been made of the Massachusetts laws of 1642 and 1647 and their Connecticut counterparts. Although they specified community responsibility and hinted at universality and compulsion at the primary level, they were far from establishing free public education in any form that we can comprehend. Indeed, it is impossible to speak of a "system" of schools, either public or private, in the colonies. An astounding percentage of persons, even in New England, received their small ration of education at home rather than in an organized school. South of Connecticut the chief agencies of education were the home, church, shop, and field. Most laws on education dealt with the special problem of preparing poor children for a gainful occupation. Free education was closely identified with poverty. This was especially true in Virginia, where the legislature enacted at least ten laws dealing with primary education of the poor, orphaned, and illegitimate.

The cultural heritage from England and the conditions of wilderness living were both unfavorable to the growth of a flourishing system of education. The class structure, the slow progress of pedagogy, political oligarchy, the high economic value placed on children, the ravages of border warfare, the dispersed pattern of rural settlement, the difficulties of transportation, the decline of learning and culture in the middle period (1675-1725), excesses of religious enthusiasm—all these were obstructions to the growth and refinement of instruments of formal education. The insatiable demands of soil and sea, which made extended leisure a will-o'-the-wisp for men of all classes, was especially responsible for the utilitarian complexion that permeated even upper-class education.

In addition to the home itself—the principal unit of primary education in all sections and among all classes—a variety of persons and institutions offered instruction in the rudiments: the semipublic writing schools of New England, the parochial schools of New York and Pennsylvania, the "old-field" schools of Virginia, and the parsons, masters, tutors, and private schools of every section. The quality of a child's education varied with his religion, class, section, and proximity to settlement. The child of an Anglican or Congregational merchant in Boston received a training far more intense than that of the child of a

Quaker farmer in Rhode Island or Calvinist family on the Virginia frontier. Yet the many instruments of primary education did have two common features: they ladled out their lessons with the spoon of authority and paid primary devotion to the five R's— Reading, 'Riting, 'Rithmetic, Rules of Virtuous Conduct, and Religion.

Comparatively few young people reached the level of education we class as secondary. Such education had two main purposes: to prepare a limited group for college and to teach a somewhat larger group the skills, learning, and manners that distinguished the merchant and planting classes from the mass of men. The chief instruments were the urban private schools, some of which became sufficiently large and stabilized to be known as "academies." The academy, a major development in eighteenth-century education, continued to offer Latin and Greek to those youths whose families intended them for college and at the same time provided a more utilitarian bill of fare— mathematics, composition, geography, modern languages, science, accounting, and bookkeeping—for those entering business and the professions. Training in good manners, genteel accomplishments, and polite learning was offered to all young men of the upper or would-be-upper class. Substantial rural families sent their sons to board in the city or employed tutors or ministers to educate them at home. Some of the best-educated men in America never saw the inside of a schoolhouse.

The colleges responded conspicuously to the pressures of a society more actively concerned than ours with religion and status. Of the seven colleges in the colonial period—Harvard (1636), William and Mary (1693), Yale (1701), New Jersey, now Princeton (1747), Philadelphia, now Pennsylvania (1749), King's, now Columbia (1754), and Rhode Island, now Brown (1764)—all but Pennsylvania were creatures of sectarian impulse, and all remained, despite the trend toward broader educational horizons, supports of the Christian order. Although then as now poor boys with talents and courage could win their way to a college education (and there, like John Wise, be lured by rich boys into extracurricular misconduct), most students were from the upper or upper-middle classes. Curriculum and methods were based on the practices of Oxford and Cambridge and thus, more remotely, on those of the great universities of medieval Europe. The ancient languages, rhetoric, and philosophy were the core of the curriculum in the early period. Mathematics, moral literature, modern languages, and science made inroads on classical subjects in the eighteenth century. The facts and fancies of political theory, history, geography, and other more worldly subjects entered the student's mind along the indirect routes of the classical writers and orthodox philosophers. Entrance into the ministry, the stated goal of a majority of students, gave a Christian cast to all parts of the curriculum.

It is easy to smile at the dull, rigid, crabbed methods that prevailed in colonial colleges, but if we judge the vineyards by the fruit they brought forth, we must acknowledge them a fertile ground of learning, science, reason, and liberty. They may not have taught young men enough useful knowledge, but they did teach them—in their own tradition-ridden way—to think, communicate, and lead. These tiny seminaries were worthy ancestors of the modern university. The roll call of Harvard and William and Mary men in the Revolution should be evidence enough that Latin, logic, and metaphysics were rich fertilizer in the cultivation of reason, virtue, honor, and love of liberty. The colleges of colonial America were well up in the movement toward a more humane and open society.

Adult education reached its peak of formal development in the seaports of the eighteenth century. Libraries circulated books among a growing proportion of the population; the books themselves grew more practical in content and instructive in method. Newspapers, of which there were none in 1700 and twenty-three in 1765, offered moral and scientific instruction as well as news of commercial and dynastic doings. Evening schools advertised courses in mathematics, navigation, surveying, bookkeeping, languages, and other useful subjects. The public lecture illustrating the magic of electricity was hardly less popular than Addison's *Cato* or Gay's *Beggar's Opera*. And as Franklin and dozens of lesser men proved conclusively, self-education in the home and club did as much as any formal institution to raise the level of knowledge and curiosity.

If there is any one phase of colonial life to which it is unwise, unjust, and unreal to apply present-day standards and values, it is the area of education. The one question we may properly ask of the total system of education is this: In the light of the environment in which it operated and the heritage upon which it was building, did it answer the needs of the people satisfactorily? The answer would seem to be an admiring yes. Despite a legion of obstacles to expansion and refinement, not the least of these being the inherent conservatism of education itself, the system was surely as good as could have been expected. Indeed, thanks to the earnest faith in education that dominated the colonial mind even in the dark days toward the end of the seventeenth century, the system could stand comparison with those of England and Europe. The vigor of this faith is one of the principal keys to the colonial mind. It was strong in 1636:

After God had carried us safe to *New-England*, and wee had builded our houses, provided necessaries for our livelihood, rear'd convenient places for Gods worship, and setled the Civill Government: One of the next things we longed

for, and looked after was to advance *Learning* and perpetu-
ate it to Posterity; dreading to leave an illiterate Ministery
to the Churches, when our present Ministers shall lie in the
Dust. And as wee were thinking and consulting how to
effect this great Work; it pleased God to stir up the heart
of one Mr. *Harvard* (a godly Gentleman, and a lover of
Learning, there living amongst us) to give the one halfe of
his Estate (it being in all about 1700. l.) towards the erect-
ing of a Colledge, and all his Library: after him another
gave 300. l. others after them cast in more, and the publique
hand of the State added the rest: The Colledge was, by
common consent, appointed to be at Cambridge, (a place
very pleasant and accomodate) and is called (according to
the name of the first founder) *Harvard Colledge*.

It was no less strong in 1754:

The Right Education of Youth has ever been esteemed,
by wise Men, one of the chief cares of the best constituted
States; and it is a Truth, confirmed both by Reason and
Experience, that *Societies* have more or less flourished, in all
that exalts or embellishes human Nature, in Proportion as
they have taken more or less Care in this important matter.

The ideals of colonial education outran the reality.
In those days, too, men lamented publicly the "contemptuous Treatment of, and parsimonious Provision
for, the Support of the Learned," and the seeming
willingness of the community "to extinguish Learning, by starving its Propagators." Yet rarely in history has a pioneer people given so much thought and
support to education. Conservative and impoverished
as the system may seem to us, it taught the mass of
men to get along on their own and the best of men
to think and lead.

III

Culture—which is defined for present purposes as the
creation, enjoyment, and criticism of literature, music, drama, and the graphic arts—was the stepchild of

colonial society. It was urban, centered for the most part in seaports like Boston and Philadelphia and capitals like Annapolis and Williamsburg; derivative, taking much of its inspiration from the culture of the mother country; passive, emphasizing enjoyment and imitation rather than creation; late-blooming, waiting perforce on the rise of an indigenous aristocracy with sufficient wealth, leisure, and aspirations to elegance; and class-conscious, supported on the narrow base of the upper and upper-middle classes. We cannot emphasize too strongly as factors in cultural development the primary role of the towns, the dominance of conscious ties with England, and the sponsorship of the merchant aristocracy. Nor should we forget, as we shake our heads over the pitifully small production of art and literature of lasting value or universal interest, the impediments that geography, religion, and the level of the economy offered to the rise of a culture worthy of the times. Most colonists would probably have agreed smugly or reluctantly with a New England author, "The Plow-man that raiseth Grain is more serviceable to Mankind, than the Painter who draws only to please the Eye. The Carpenter who builds a good House to defend us from the Wind and Weather, is more serviceable than the curious Carver, who employs his Art to please the Fancy."

Prose and poetry, especially when instructive and inspirational, were both held in high esteem throughout the colonial period. Printing houses grew ever more numerous and productive. By the middle of the eighteenth century some twenty presses were printing several hundred separate titles and nearly twenty newspapers and magazines a year, all of which led one cynic to observe, "Letters (I don't mean Learning) grow upon us daily." Books and periodicals were imported in astounding numbers from England, and booksellers and subscription libraries did a thriving business. The Library Company of Philadelphia, the Charleston Library Society, and the New York Society Library were the most successful examples of a movement that did much to lift the level of culture and understanding in the colonies. Private libraries, too, played an essential part in this advance, for in a pioneer society eager for knowledge the lending of books was a public duty. Franklin's tribute to the colonial libraries is well worth hearing:

These libraries have improved the general conversation of the Americans, made the common tradesmen and farmers as intelligent as most gentlemen from other countries, and perhaps have contributed in some degree to the stand so generally made throughout the colonies in defence of their privileges.

Theological disputation, the classics, history, moral essays, and heroic verse were the forms of literature most enthusiastically imported and enjoyed. Although it is impossible to judge the popularity of each of the scores of English, Continental, and classical authors whose works appear repeatedly in library lists, wills, and advertisements, we can say with certainty that the urban culture of the eighteenth century prized two writers above all others: Joseph Addison (and to a lesser extent Richard Steele) for *The Spectator*, Alexander Pope for *An Essay on Man*. Both the style and content of these products of eighteenth-century England appealed strongly to the colonial mind. The prose of *The Spectator* and poetry of the *Essay on Man* were the arbiters of style. When newspapers were not filled with excerpts from these authors, they were overfilled with essays imitative of the one and verse imitative of the other. The *Essay on Man* was reprinted in America five times before 1765. Bacon, Locke, Butler, Shakespeare, Bunyan, Milton, Watts, Defoe, Swift, Dryden, Burnet, Richardson, Dodsley, and Smollett were perhaps the next most popular literary figures. Montaigne,

Voltaire, Buffon, Rabelais, and Montesquieu all won substantial followings, but the most popular single item of French origin was Fénelon's *Télémaque,* a political novel advertising the doctrine that kings exist for people rather than people for kings.

The bulk of the literature produced by the colonists themselves consisted of theological tracts, political pamphlets, and histories. Jonathan Edwards and John Woolman did the best-remembered work in the first category, although the fantastic outpourings of the Mathers and their colleagues can also be panned for a few semiprecious gems. Political pamphleteering became a popular pastime in the eighteenth century, reaching its artistic zenith in the tracts of the Revolution. The works of Bradford, Winthrop, Johnson, Mather, Prince, Stith, Byrd, Beverley, Smith, Douglass, Colden, and Hutchinson form a highly respectable body of historical literature. Several of these histories were published in colonial times to edify and inspire the colonists themselves. The majestic theme of the American Mission raises some of them to heights of colonial self-consciousness not reached in any other branch of our early literature. As to poets, the colonies spawned dozens of imitators of Pope like Mather Byles and producers of doggerel like Michael Wigglesworth, but not one who could be taken seriously in England. Anne Bradstreet, Edward Taylor of Massachusetts, the unknown author of "Bacon's Epitaph," and Francis Hopkinson of Philadelphia are the most interesting representatives of the handful of poets who receive passing mention in modern anthologies.

The literature of early America was wholly a product of men busy with the affairs of life. No man of letters earned his bread in the colonies. Yet for all the stultifying effects of environment and dependence, a literature of astonishing quantity and at least respectable quality did manage to flourish. In Franklin's descriptions of his experiments, Byrd's entertaining comments on the men of the frontier, and the "captive narratives" of plain people like Mary Rowlandson the beginnings of a true American literature are plainly visible. Historians of our literature have no cause to apologize for the colonial period.

Music as an art labored under discouraging handicaps. Not until well into the eighteenth century were the tastes and fortunes of any group of colonists sufficiently advanced to promote the staging of a formal concert; the first such affair took place under Anglican auspices, and amid prophecies of hellfire, in Boston in 1731. Well before this date, especially in the more easygoing and gentle-minded South, a few men of polite aspirations were performing, bravely if not professionally, on imported instruments in their own homes. As the eighteenth century progressed, private enjoyment and public performance both quickened noticeably. The latter was largely confined to urban centers, where the composers in favor in London were treated with respect if not entire fidelity. American composers did not exist. The sonatas of Scarlatti and suites of Handel vied with the ever-welcome *Beggar's Opera* for first rank in cultivated hearts. The peak of artistic performance and popular enjoyment was reached among the Germans, especially in the Moravian settlement at Bethlehem. Yet a high wall of cultural isolation separated these people from the aristocracy of the urban centers. The laboriously imitative chamber concerts staged in the governor's palace at Williamsburg were unfortunately more representative of the quality and popularity of serious music in colonial America.

The theater was, if anything, even more dependent on alien plays and players for the modest success it achieved. The old prejudices against the drama, like those against music and dancing, gave way slowly in some places and not at all in others. In this instance, too, the English-conscious gentry of the cities led the way in defying an active tradition that exulted in the absence of "Masquerades, Plays, Balls, Midnight Revellings or Assemblies to Debauch the Mind or promote Intrigue." Despite the deep hostility that continued well past 1765 in Quaker-Presbyterian Philadelphia and Puritan Boston, the theater took strong hold in the few places that could support it. New York, Charleston, and Williamsburg were treated to isolated performances and "seasons." Shakespeare (unadulterated or "altered by Colly Cibber, Esq."), Steele, Rowe, Lillo, Congreve, Farquhar, Garrick, Gay, Dryden, and Otway were all welcomed with acclaim, but Addison's *Cato*, which appealed to Whiggish hearts even more strongly than Fénelon's *Télémaque*, was the favorite of American audiences. Thomas Godfrey, Jr.'s *Prince of Parthia*, which was presented at Philadelphia in 1767, was the first American play to be performed in public. It was noticeably faithful to English models in form, plot, language, and mood. And although colonists staged amateur plays in club, home, and college, and filled minor roles in professional productions, the best roles in the best performances were spoken by Englishmen. The traveling company of Englishmen organized by Lewis Hallam and continued by David Douglass was the one bright ornament of the colonial theater. Douglass fooled no one but the patriots when he changed the name of his troupe to "The American Company" in 1766.

Far less dependent and derivative than the theater, and therefore more successful in expressing creative impulses in the colonial mind, was the art of painting. Many painters in the colonies, such as Smibert, Theus, and Hesselius, were transplanted Europeans;

many more were native limners who were willing
slaves to the latest English style. Yet in Robert Feke,
Benjamin West, John Singleton Copley, and Charles
Willson Peale the colonies bred artists of genuine
merit. In his American phase Copley raised the genre
of bourgeois realism to a high level of beauty and maturity. He was unquestionably early America's most
notable artistic genius. Yet his removal to England
is more instructive for our purposes than a critical
appraisal of *Mrs. Michael Gill* or the wonderful *Boy
with Squirrel*. Early American painting was for the
most part portrait painting under the sponsorship of
the aristocracy, and far too much of it was in an in-
appropriate "court style." The limits of such sponsorship were plainly too narrow for men with the
genius of Copley and West. America could not yet
give the artist enough of the things he needed except majestic themes and the exciting sense of identification with a brave new world. Yet in cutting
himself loose from his native surroundings, each of
these estimable painters may have lost his chance for
universal acclaim.

American architecture was peculiarly the prisoner
of England. Except for Peter Harrison of Newport,
himself an immigrant from England, the colonies did
not produce a single architect who could challenge
the dictatorial sway of the construction guides of
Englishmen like Inigo Jones and James Gibbs. On the
frontier and among the plain people architecture
could be functional, shrewd, and expressive of solid
values. But wherever wealth accumulated and men aspired, deliberate imitation of English patterns was the
rule. The great houses of the eighteenth-century aristocracy were almost all Georgian. The Warner house
in Portsmouth and Hammond house in Annapolis are
visible reminders that while the taste of our ancestors was good as far as it went, it went straight
to England whenever it had the chance. If there is

much that is American about Nassau Hall and West-over, there is much more that is English.

A word might be added about the minor arts in America. The range of imaginative power and degree of technical skill necessary to produce lasting achievements in the primary arts could not yet grow in American soil, but in such crafts as furniture-making and silversmithing colonial craftsmen, once again following the lead if not the dictation of English masters, achieved a high level of professional competence. The cabinetmakers and silversmiths of Philadelphia could have made a handsome living in London. An insight into the character and aspirations of colonial society is provided by the fact that these creators of objects both useful and beautiful were rewarded with large incomes and high social standing.

The folk culture of the colonies was more legend than fact. Honest searchers for genuine examples of colonial folk art—whether in furniture, sign painting, balladry, gravestones, or frontier narratives—are generally certain to meet frustration. Except among the culturally isolated Germans of the western valleys the art, music, and literature of the people was extremely sterile. Much has been made of the almanacs of Franklin, Ames, and their lesser imitators as vehicles of folk culture, but only by those who confuse instruction with creation. The almanacs are a phenomenon of early American mass culture that deserve the attention they get, but as media dispensing the imported wisdom of Newton and secular morality of Franklin downward to the plain people rather than channeling the native wisdom of the plain people upward to the cultivated world. In time the almanacs became small magazines that offered lectures on astronomy, practical hints on farming, political thoughts, capsuled history, jokes, poems, recipes, distance tables, medical advice, moral essays, and calculations. The almanac was, next to the Bible, the most active ingredient in the culture of the people; as such it provides a rewarding glimpse of the practicality and sterility of the mass mind.

The culture of the colonies, like that of later America, was a jumble of contradictions: good taste, bad taste, and no taste at all; slavish imitation, intelligent selection, and bold experiment; erudition, common sense, and base ignorance. The creation of an indigenous culture was regarded as the next task of this ingenious people, yet it was already being argued that they would be led astray rather than set free by the accumulation of surplus capital. Liberty, respect for learning and artistic achievement, and the broadening of educational opportunity were factors highly favorable to the building of an American culture, but materialism had already begun its tireless assault on sound values and the creative impulse. "The only principle of Life propagated among the young People is to get Money," growled Cadwallader Colden in 1748, "and Men are only esteemed according to . . . the Money they are possessed of." The struggle of the artist and scholar to gain the respect and encouragement of their fellow citizens was already under way in the colonial period.

IV

The colonial mind had a peculiar respect and affinity for science. The opening of America to settlement and the birth of modern science were cognate developments of Western civilization. Science and its philosophical corollaries were perhaps the most important intellectual force shaping the destiny of eighteenth-century America, and the men of America were quick to acknowledge and eager to repay the debt. It is not entirely coincidental that in this instance the westward current of ideas should have been at least partially reversed. Colonial influence on English and European thought scored its one modest success in the field of science. The reasons for the vigor of colonial science are not easy to unravel, but it is possible to point to the overpowering presence of nature, the practical needs of the colonists, and the fascination of the natural world for minds grown weary of the supernatural as factors that recommended it strongly to Americans of all classes and sections.

Science in colonial America was Newtonian science, an inquiry into the phenomena of the natural world in the spirit and with the methods of Sir Isaac Newton. The influence of this great man, which extended well beyond the bounds of science, was a determining element in the relationship of the colonial mind to the world about it. Through Newton's writings the new approach to nature of Bacon, Copernicus, Harvey, Kepler, Brahe, Galileo, Descartes, and Boyle was impressed on colonial understanding. Few colonists ever so much as saw the cover of the *Principia*, but the assumptions and attitudes of Newtonian science, made palatable to the learned few in dozens of explanatory books and to the people in almanacs and newspapers, took strong hold upon their imaginations. As Carl Becker has written, "It was not necessary to read the *Principia* in order to be a good Newtonian, any more than it is necessary to read the *Origin of Species* in order to be a good Darwinian." Empiricism, rationalism, induction, the mechanical explanation of natural phenomena—all these techniques and postulates of the new science found favor in the inquiring colonial mind. And since Newton insisted stubbornly that he had come not to destroy but to fulfill the teachings of revealed religion, Cotton Mather could take him to his bosom no less warmly than Franklin or Colden. Mather extended Newton the ultimate accolade when he called him "the perpetual Dictator of the learned World." Most Americans were ready to sing right along with William Livingston to

> IMMORTAL NEWTON; whose illustrious name
> Will shine on records of eternal fame.

Science in the colonies was divided into two broad categories: natural philosophy, in which physics and astronomy were the most important special fields, and natural history, in which botany aroused the keenest interest. The mind of the colonial scientist was not given to making careful distinctions; the man we now remember for work in electricity or astronomy was probably no less concerned with botany, medicine, mechanics, and meteorology. Students of the colonial mind must use modern divisions and subdivisions of science with extreme care, for the ideal of the "whole man," certainly in the field of science, still had meaning in the eighteenth century.

A goodly company of Americans made contributions to the accumulating body of knowledge of the natural world. The leading man of colonial science was, of course, Benjamin Franklin, whose work in electricity, oceanography, meteorology, and physics brought him the respect of the learned few and plaudits of the unlearned many in England, France, and America. Franklin was always quick to acknowledge the co-operation and discoveries of the many other Americans with whom he worked and corresponded. John Winthrop of Harvard, second only to Franklin in the muster of colonial scientists, repaid his debt to Newton with brilliant work in astronomy and sound investigation in a half-dozen other fields. Thomas Brattle of Harvard, some of whose observations were used by Newton in the *Principia*, and David Rittenhouse of Philadelphia, whose orreries at Princeton and Philadelphia were wonders of the age, were other pioneers in a field that had a strong ap-

peal for colonial minds. Electricity, hardly less popular than astronomy after the diffusion of Franklin's
experiments, numbered such votaries as James Bowdoin of Boston, John Lining of Charleston, Philip
Syng of Franklin's Junto, and Ebenezer Kinnersley,
the popularizer of electrical knowledge. All these men
were willing workers in other vineyards of natural
philosophy. Franklin had a correspondent worthy of
his fellowship in Cadwallader Colden, the nearest
thing to the whole man New York has ever shel-
tered. Colden, who turned his hand to at least as
many divisions of science as Franklin, is of particular
interest as the first scientific mind in America more
devoted to theory than to practical experiment. His
ambitious *Principles of Action in Matter*, which was
published in America, England, and on the Continent,
was a bold if bewildering attempt to enlarge upon
Newton.

Natural history attracted several first-rate minds.
John Clayton's *Flora Virginia*, Jared Eliot's experiments in scientific agriculture, James Logan's study
of sex in plants, Alexander Garden's classification of
plants, and above all John Bartram's work in collection and cross-fertilization were contributions to
botany that received the acclaim of the best European natural scientists. William Douglass, John Banis-
ter, William Byrd II, Dr. John Mitchell, and Colden
were all close observers of the flora of the new world.
Douglass, Winthrop, and others looked hard for the
natural causes of earthquakes. Bartram, Colden,
Mitchell, and Lewis Evans pioneered in descriptive
anthropology. Medicine, a time-honored battlefield of
superstitious traditionalism and scientific procedure,
made few advances in the colonies, and most of these
were the work of men trained in Europe. John Tennent, Zabdiel Boylston, Colden, Garden, Lining,
Douglass, Mitchell, John Kearsley, Thomas Bond, and
John Morgan were men whose knowledge and meth-

ods were more prophetic than typical. It has been estimated that only 200 out of 3,500 persons practicing medicine in the colonies just before the Revolution had medical degrees, and little that even these 200 advised would be classed today as sound medicine. The men who have been mentioned here were only the most prominent of colonial scientists. Dozens of other searchers of the wonders of the world, from John Winthrop, Jr., of Connecticut through Thomas Robie of Harvard to William Small of William and Mary, are also due a measure of credit for the development of this uniquely successful branch of learning.

Whatever the object of their inquiries and however primitive their methods, colonial scientists had three traits in common: They showed a special interest in the world immediately about them. whether it took the form of rattlesnakes, corn, lightning, Indians, or earthquakes; they were, with one or two obvious exceptions like Colden the theorist and Bartram the pure lover of nature, utilitarian in outlook or motivation, hoping consciously with Franklin that their work would prove a "benefit of mankind in general"; and they were imbued with the spirit of the new science, with the conviction that openminded observation was the only technique with which to come to grips with nature. Their knowledge of mathematical tools may have been limited and their hypotheses few, but they were an enthusiastic band of brothers in their devotion to nature and her laws. Another characteristic common to most colonial scientists was the pursuit of full careers in other fields. Bartram was able to support himself by selling plants and seeds to other botanists; Winthrop, Small, and Isaac Greenwood of Harvard earned livelihoods as teachers. The others were at best what we would call elegant amateurs.

Only a small fraction of the advances in science

registered in this era were inspired or supported by the colleges. Yet the colleges were unusually friendly to science. Even in the seventeenth century Harvard was offering some instruction in natural philosophy; there is evidence that Copernicus had conquered the young Turks of the faculty as early as 1659. Late in the century began a shift to the new science that was brought to a revolutionary if somewhat alcoholic climax in the professorship of Isaac Greenwood (1727-1738). While Harvard and William and Mary led the way, the others were not far behind. By 1750 science claimed a sizable portion of the student's time at each of the old colleges, and at the Philadelphia Academy he might be giving up to 40 per cent of his hours to mathematics, physics, mechanics, astronomy, botany, agriculture, and other scientific studies. The methods of teaching were dull, primitive, and didactic by modern standards, but they were well on the road to liberation from the scholastic past. Jefferson's tribute to William Small—"To his enlightened and affectionate guidance of my studies while at college, I am indebted for everything"—was also a tribute to academic science in the colonies. If it did little to discover, it did much to receive, disseminate, and inspire.

The Royal Society of London extended welcome assistance to colonial science. The leadership of this great institution reminds us that the eminence of American science was only relative, that in this area, too, the colonies were still a provincial outpost of European learning. The learned society rather than the college was the key institution in the advance of scientific learning in the Age of the Enlightenment, and the fact that colonists like Franklin were willing but unable to inaugurate and maintain a genuine learned society before 1765 is evidence of a people not yet ready for intellectual independence. In the absence of a colonial corresponding society, the

Royal Society was the channel through which new discoveries and hypotheses were sped to America and American contributions were advertised to England and the continent. The *Philosophical Transactions* carried several score important papers originating in the colonies, and eighteen Americans were elected to fellowship in the Society before 1776.

The currents of science flowing in from England and Europe and the freshets of science arising in the colonies gave a notable swell to the ongoing stream of political liberty. The new freedom in science and the new freedom in government were, of course, collateral developments in the unfolding of the Enlightenment. It would be hard to say which freedom, political or scientific, was more instrumental in fostering the other, but we may point to at least three ways in which Newtonian science quickened the advance toward free government. First, it helped break down the wall of superstition and ignorance that blocked the road to the open society. We have learned already of the importance of humanistic religion in the rise of political liberty; the new science was historically and logically a major element in this religion. The repressive alliance of authoritarian religion and the monolithic state fought savagely, but in vain, against the massive infiltration of the new alliance of science, rationalism, and libertarian political thought. In America as in Europe science released men's minds from bondage to the "false truths of revelation," then encouraged these minds to believe that truth, in any field of human endeavor, could be discovered by impartial observation and fearless application of reason. A decisive majority of the best minds in eighteenth-century America considered the use of reason an essential prop of free government, and science had done as much as any other intellectual force to advertise the beauties—and limits—of reason to their minds.

The advance of science popularized other methods and assumptions that were essential to the conduct of free government. Franklin was only one of a number of forward-looking colonists who recognized the kinship of scientific method and democratic procedure. Free inquiry, free exchange of information, optimism, self-criticism, pragmatism, objectivity—all these ingredients of the coming republic were already active in the republic of science that flourished in the eighteenth century.

Finally, the new science had a direct influence on the development of American political and constitutional thought. Basic to the Newtonian system were the grand generalizations of a universe governed by immutable natural laws and of harmony as the pattern and product of these laws. The first of these gave new sanction to the doctrine of natural law; the second had much to do with the growing popularity of the Whiggish principle of balanced government. It is going a bit too far to look upon the American Constitution as a monument to Sir Isaac Newton, but certainly the widespread acceptance of his theory of a harmonious universe helped create an intellectual atmosphere in which a system of checks and balances would have a special appeal to constitution-makers. If John Winthrop could thank immortal Newton for discovering the law of attraction and repulsion, "the fundamental law which the alwise CREATOR has established for regulating the several movements in this grand machine," certainly John Adams could thank him for supporting the law of checks and balances, the fundamental law of the machine of constitutional government.

I do not mean to overstate either the progress or influence of colonial science. America produced no Newton or Boyle, and science was but one of many intellectual forces that encouraged men to think in terms of human liberty. Yet we cannot ignore the

influence of the scientific spirit in generating an attitude of optimism and open-mindedness, an attitude
that the almanacs and newspapers helped to spread
among the plain people. Science had done much to
improve man's lot, and the end was by no means in
sight. The feeling of pride in the advances of the age
and of confidence in the ages yet to come was best
expressed by an anonymous writer in the *Virginia
Gazette:*

So vast are the Improvements of Sciences, that all our
Knowledge of Mathematics, of Nature, of the brightest Part
of humane Wisdom, had their Admission among us within
the last two Centuries. . . . The World is now daily increasing in experimental Knowledge, and let no Man flatter
the Age, with pretending we are arrived to a Perfection of
Discoveries.

V

Philosophy in the formal sense hardly existed at all in
colonial America. Those men with enough learning
to think philosophically were too much concerned
with theological disputation or the affairs of life to
help build up an environment in which a Hobbes or
Locke, or even a Shaftesbury or Berkeley, could arise
and prosper. Dr. Samuel Johnson of Connecticut was
a devoted exponent of Berkeley's subjective idealism;
his *Elementa Philosophia*, written for his students at
King's, was the only formal defense of a philosophical
system produced in the colonies. Cadwallader Colden
wrote a number of books and letters in which he
came close to a philosophy of pure materialism. In his
ever-charming *Journal* John Woolman brought mysticism to a pitch of intensity rarely if ever matched
in this country. And Jonathan Edwards, in his defense
of the old faith, worked out a memorable exposition
of unreconstructed Puritanism touched with idealism and mysticism. But these were at best the

gropings for truth of men who, except for Johnson, cannot be considered philosophers in the technical sense.

Philosophy in the broader sense of an outlook on life or a system of practical ethics found a happy home in the colonial mind. Most educated colonists seem to have searched consciously for fixed principles of moral wisdom, and many of little or no education also had a "philosophy" of their own. Three patterns of thought claim the attention of the student of the colonial mind: Puritanism, rationalism, and middle-class morality. Most men of standing in early America subscribed to one or another, or to a prudent combination, of these working philosophies. All were highly derivative in character, finding their law and prophets in the mother country. All had a formative impact on the developing American mind and thus upon the rise of liberty.

The Puritan way of life is an earnest reminder that religion, especially the Christian religion as it emerged from the magnificent mind of John Calvin, was the dominant element in the working philosophies of most colonists. Puritanism as a way of life was in its prime an extension of a system of theology that held to the austere doctrines of an unknowable and omnipotent God who intervenes constantly in the unfolding of nature and lives of men; of men corrupt and depraved, for whom salvation through grace was the only need and goal; of a world created from nothing and destined for nothing; and of truth as a gift of God to be received through revelation rather than reason. The triumph of orthodox Puritanism as a theology was the signal of its failure as a way of life. It embraced too much, it dug too deep, it speculated too minutely. It made too much of piety among a people quite unready to renounce the world. Yet "reconstructed Puritanism," the less austere but highly moralistic brand of practical ethics that developed in the colonies, was a leading way of life in eighteenth-century America.

The moral teachings of Puritanism, the principles of individual conduct that it pressed so insistently upon unregenerate man, were just those rules one might expect to hear proclaimed by a Christian movement burning to reform the world yet live in it. Piety, sobriety, industry, honesty, frugality, simplicity, order, silence, resolution—these were the instrumental virtues through which men might yet build here on earth a reasonable imitation of the city of God. The practice of them brought Puritan saints no nearer to the arbitrarily bestowed gift of salvation and eternal life, but the man who displayed them in his dealings with other men could consider himself an expediter of God's great plan to reform the world. And although he could not in his orthodoxy subscribe to a covenant of works, it was hard for the good Puritan to believe that he was predestined to eternal torment. The virtuous life was, if not the means, certainly the sign of salvation, and the practice of the Puritan virtues became in itself a consuming purpose.

Both as theology and way of life Puritanism was constantly in evolution. Perhaps the most interesting development, or rather pair of developments, was the splitting of its apparent monolith into the neo-orthodoxy of Jonathan Edwards and Thomas Clap, sons of austere Yale, and the Christian rationalism of Jonathan Mayhew and Charles Chauncy, sons of latitudinarian Harvard. These two lines of development in Puritan thought can be traced back to the dichotomy of revelation and reason in the systems of the great saints like Thomas Hooker and John Cotton, to the decisive fact of intellectual history that the Puritans, scholastics all, were anxious to demonstrate logically the coherency and consistency of revealed dogma. In seeking to bolster revelation with reason, to make a philosophy out of piety, they laid open their whole rugged creed to the incursions of rationalism. The liberal theology and moral teachings of Mayhew were as legitimate descendants of seventeenth-century Puritanism as were the magnificent apologia of Edwards or the reactionary gospel of Clap. Thanks to its historic insistence on reason and disapproval of enthusiasm, Puritanism moved into enlightened rationalism more gracefully and naturally than any other denomination in the Protestant left wing.

The plans of the Puritan fathers for a holy commonwealth in the new world never did stand much chance of success. The wilderness environment was a treacherous foundation, the men of the great migration defective materials. Yet the Puritan system of practical ethics, which called upon responsible, rational, virtuous, self-reliant men to pursue their busy lives within a system of ordered liberty, was the first and, it may certainly be argued, the greatest of all American ways of life.

Rationalism was a way of thinking that cherished reason as the path to valid knowledge; assumed the worth and dignity of man, as well as his ability to use reason in the search for happiness and truth; proclaimed a benevolent, dependable, gentlemanly God; and therefore stood forth in its most developed form as an enlightened protest against tradition, dogma, superstition, and authority. Rationalism moved into the colonial consciousness on the heels of Newtonian science, but it found the ground already prepared for it by Puritanism and Anglicanism. The colonial rationalists found their chief sources of inspiration among men of the latter faith: in the writings of such latitudinarians as John Tillotson, Archbishop of Canterbury; Samuel Clarke and William Wollaston, Anglican ministers; and John Locke and Sir Isaac Newton, by their own admission devoted sons of the Church. Those who went one step further with Lord

Shaftesbury and Anthony Collins to deprive religion entirely of dependence on revelation were dangerously near to all-out deism, but this logical extension of the rationalist position made slow headway among the conservative and practical-minded colonists. Rationalism in colonial America was Christian rationalism, not least because the rich and well-born to whom these ideas appealed were unwilling to sap the most solid foundation of a stable society. Even so skeptical a thinker as Franklin thought organized Christianity a necessary support of free and ordered government. And no prominent colonial thinker went overboard in his faith in reason.

Rationalism, like its offspring deism, was more class-conscious than most other systems of thought: It made its deepest inroads into the educated upper class, which was also, be it noted, the carrier of Newtonian science. It made hardly any impression at all on the mass of men, for whom tradition, superstition, and indifference remained determining intellectual influences. The planters, merchants, and liberal preachers who welcomed rationalism to their bosoms were leaders in action as well as thought, and through their good offices rationalism worked considerable influence on the colonial mind. First, it helped liberalize all those religions, especially Congregationalism and Anglicanism, which made room for reason. Second, as the creed of men who labored the distinction between the religion of the Gospels and that of the priests, it reintroduced the moral teachings of Jesus to many upper-class minds. By elevating reason into "an universal rule, as well in religious, as civil affairs," it played a part in ridding educated minds of dependence on tradition and dogma. Next, it gave added impetus to the upward trend of humanitarianism, for it was impressed if not obsessed with the notion that wicked institutions prevent the flowering of the decency inherent in all men. So far as the rationalist was concerned, the most acceptable service to God was kindness to God's children. Fifth, since it drew much of its inspiration from the Newtonian concept of a harmonious universe governed by immutable laws, it advertised the notions of mechanistic society and balanced government, both of them corollaries of the doctrine of higher law. Finally, rationalism placed emphasis on virtuous living and thus contributed to the vogue of morality and moralizing in eighteenth-century America. Most colonial rationalists would have agreed with an author in the Boston *American Magazine* that reason was "speculative Virtue" and virtue "practical Reason."

Few people in history have been more given to public moralizing, to proclaiming a catalogue of virtues and exhorting one another to exhibit them, than the American colonists. Practical morality was an important by-product of Puritanism and rationalism as well as of the actual experiences of the colonists. Yet so prevalent was this pattern of thought, so universal and self-generating was the urge to preach the solid virtues, that we may consider it an independent working philosophy to which thousands of colonists subscribed directly. I have prefixed the adjective "middle-class" because the virtues most loudly sung and vices most loudly damned were those that the man "on the make," the man so representative of eighteenth-century America, would be especially eager to display or shun. Even the conscious Virginia aristocrat, the devoted reader of Allestree's *A Gentleman's Calling* and Peacham's *The Compleat Gentleman*, was infected with the desire to preach and practice virtues that a genuine Cavalier would have refused to admit to his list.

A thorough check of newspapers and magazines, the chief purveyors of this morality, shows these virtues to have been the most repeatedly discussed:

wisdom, justice, temperance, fortitude, industry, frugality, piety, charity, sobriety, sincerity, honesty, simplicity, humility, contentment, love, benevolence, humanity, mercy, patriotism, modesty, patience, and good manners. The columns of newspapers in every part of the colonies were filled with original essays, letters, and London reprints praising one, several, or all of these virtues. The virtues themselves, as can be plainly seen, were an ill-assorted mishmash of Greek, Roman, Christian, and latter-day English qualities, some of them ends and others means, some of them gentle and others quite vulgar in origin and appeal. The vices most often warned against were, of course, the opposites of the cherished virtues: ignorance, injustice, intemperance, cowardice, laziness, luxury, irreverence, selfishness, drunkenness, deceit, fraud, covetousness, vanity, ambition, hate, violence, flattery, ingratitude, and bad manners. The regularity and virulence with which authors assaulted these vices is evidence enough that middle-class morality was more an ideal than a reality in the colonies.

Just how a man was to practice the one and shun the other was never made clear in these thousands of essays. Just why he should do so was proclaimed again and again by imitators of Addison, Pope, Mather, and Franklin: because at the end of the high road of virtue lay the precious goals of individual freedom and national well-being, of liberty and prosperity for a man and his country. By such well-worn devices as the horrible example, the dream, the success story, the portrayal of the good and honest man, the appeal to ancient Rome (the "most virtuous Country which ever existed"), the Greek or Roman oration, and the straightforward promise of prosperity, the men of America bid one another be good.

The ultimate sanction of virtue, to which the moralist appealed repeatedly, was religion. Few men who cherished virtue as the foundation of liberty ever doubted that religion was in turn the foundation of virtue. Said a favorite London reprint:

Remember, Posterity! that Virtue is the Soul of Liberty, and Religion is the Soul of Virtue; and therefore, to see a People, whose Virtue is departed, exert the Powers invested in them by their Laws, for the Defence of Liberty, would be to the full as great a Miracle, as if a rotten Carcase, the Relic of a departed Soul should rise up, and, unanimated by its former Inhabitant, perform the ordinary Functions of Life. So that if you will be free, you must be virtuous; and if you will be virtuous, you must be religious. Let me then most seriously and earnestly recommend to you, the earliest and most careful Instruction of Youth, in the Belief of God and the Christian Religion.

Virtue was hardly less dependent on the diffusion of knowledge:

It has been the constant Observation in all Ages and Nations, that as *Learning* and *Knowledge* increased, so did the *Vertue, Strength* and *Liberty* of the People; and where the same has decreased by the like Degrees, the People have degenerated into *Vice, Poverty,* and *Slavery. Ease* and *Plenty* are the natural Fruits of *Liberty;* and where these abound, *Learning* and the liberal Arts flourish.

We may smile, we may weary at the endless moralizing of the colonists, but there can be no doubt that here was a practical philosophy of huge consequence for the American future.

The common elements in these philosophies account for their peculiar appeal to the developing American mind. From reconstructed Puritanism, from Christian rationalism, and from the morality of the rising middle class the colonist learned most of the valuable lessons that he was also learning, if he were any sort of pragmatist, from his efforts to get along in the American environment. All these philosophies sang of individualism, reason, self-improvement, activity, and a religion of good works; all **were** optimistic about man's nature and the nation's future; all were moralistic, and the morality they preached had its reward in this world as well as in the next; and all rejected the notion of infallibility in religion and politics, exalting in its place the great right of private judgment. The ways of life that held sway in the colonial period were uniquely suited to the needs of an upstart people more intent upon pursuing happiness than storming the gates of Heaven.

VI

Economic and social theory, which I touched upon in Chapters II and V, were fields of speculation to which few colonists were attracted. The thinking American had little time or use for economic theory; unlike many of his twentieth-century descendants, he was not given to asserting that political liberty depended upon the existence of one particular economic system. His social theory was simply a bundle of unproved assumptions about social stratification, the patriarchal family, female inferiority, and the general hopelessness of improving the lot of the poor, sick, depraved, and enslaved. Economic and social theory both remained at a primitive level throughout the colonial period.

It was quite otherwise with political theory. If the seventeenth century had been an age of theology, the eighteenth was an age of politics. The pace of public life was slow; indifference rather than eager participation marked the average man's attitude toward government. Yet there were incidents —the founding of an unorthodox newspaper in Boston, the trial of a popular editor in New York, an attack on an unpopular proprietary government in Pennsylvania, an arbitrary levying of a land fee in Virginia—that touched off political controversies of an intensely partisan nature. Men of opposing views rushed boldly into the lists, and arguments over specific issues were supported by appeals to general principles. The resulting pamphlets, broadsides, and newspaper articles reveal that the thinking men of eighteenth-century America were peculiarly at home in political disputation. They reveal, too, the astonishing distance the colonial mind had traveled since the logic-chopping days of the New England saints. Theology still held prime interest for many colonists, as Dr. Hamilton of Maryland learned in a Connecticut tavern:

After dinner there came in a rabble of clowns who fell to disputing upon points of divinity as learnedly as if they had been professed theologues. 'Tis strange to see how this humour prevails, even among the lower class of the people here. They will talk so pointedly about justification, sanctification, adoption, regeneration, repentance, free grace, reprobation, original sin, and a thousand other such pritty, chimerical knick knacks as if they had done nothing but studied divinity all their life time and perused all the lumber of the scholastic divines, and yet the fellows look as much, or rather more, like clowns than the very riffraff of our Maryland planters.

But the colonist who counted, the preacher or merchant or planter who led his fellows in thought and action, devoted a healthy portion of his speculative moments to politics and political man. The leading figures in political thought were educated men in the upper and upper-middle classes: the prophetic preachers of New England, the contentious merchants and lawyers of the middle colonies, and the less articulate but no less mettlesome planters of the South. The result of this monopoly of political disputation by men of affairs was a political theory more imitative than original, more opportunistic than profound, more propagandistic than speculative. The chief printed sources—the Massachusetts and Connecticut election sermons, the tracts of politically oriented preachers like John Wise and Jonathan Mayhew, the essays and letters in such alert journals as the *New-England Courant* (1721-1722), *New-York Weekly Journal* (1733-1736), *Boston Independent Advertiser* (1748-1749), and *Independent Reflector* (1752-1753), and the pamphlets and public letters of secular thinkers like Daniel Dulany, Richard Bland, Joseph Galloway, Benjamin Franklin, and William Livingston—show that political thought was the handmaiden of political action. The mission of colonial America was to carry a political tradition to conclusion, not to create a tradition of its own.

Political thought in the colonies was a proudly conscious extension of political thought in England. The more independent and self-assertive the colonists became, the more anxious they were to sound like trueborn Englishmen. The prophets to whom appeals for support were most often and confidently directed were John Locke, Algernon Sidney, Lord Bolingbroke, John Somers, Benjamin Hoadly, Henry Care, James Burgh, Addison, Pope, and the estimable team of Thomas Gordon and John Trenchard. Americans were not in the habit of appealing to Americans, and Continental publicists like Grotius and Vattel and classical authorities like Plutarch and Cicero were valued chiefly as scouts for the English Whigs. The colonists stood, especially in their reception of natural law, at the end of a line of speculative development more than two thousand years old. They could very easily have imported all their essential theoretical notions straight from the Continent. The most attractive political thinker of the middle period, John Wise of Ipswich, found most of his explosive ideas in the *De Jure Naturae* of Baron Pufendorf. But most colonists preferred to go to the English writers in the Whig tradition for their lessons in political theory. Locke, Bolingbroke, Sidney, Addison, and Gordon and Trenchard were, so far as the colonists were concerned, the great men of this tradition, and the greatest of these were Gordon and Trenchard. No one can spend any time in the newspapers, library inventories, and pamphlets of colonial America without realizing that *Cato's Letters* rather than Locke's *Civil Government* was the most popular, quotable, esteemed source of political ideas in the colonial period. The uncompromising Whiggery of "the Divine English Cato" was well calculated to stir colonial hearts. So long as Americans were more concerned with English rights than natural rights, Gordon and Trenchard were the witnesses most repeatedly called upon to support colonial pretensions to liberty.

The appeal of Gordon, Trenchard, Locke, and the other defenders of English liberty was in no sense a narrow one. Except for a few lonely votaries of Tory conservatism, colonists of every political shade were dedicated wholeheartedly to the English constitutional tradition. Conservatives, middle-of-the-roaders, and radicals hammered at one another with the slogans of Whiggery. Rarely if ever in the history of free government has there been so unanimous a "party line" as that to which the colonists pledged their uncritical allegiance. And rarely if ever has the party line been so easily reduced to one comprehensible concept, even to one wonderful word: *Liberty*. Liberty, defined simply and unanimously as that "which exempts one Man from Subjection to another, so far as the Order and Oeconomy of Government will permit," was the undefiled darling of colonial political thought. The fact that little attempt was made to go any further with this definition, except to make pious distinctions between liberty and license, served only to strengthen the notion that liberty was the ultimate value toward which political speculation should be directed. One of the authors of the *Independent Reflector* spoke for almost all colonial thinkers when he adopted as his "principal Design . . . opposing Oppression, and vindicating the *Liberty of Man.*"

In colonial as in English political thought the edifice of liberty was made to rest on three grand supports: natural law and natural rights, Whig constitutionalism, and virtue. The ancient doctrine of natural law and its latter-day corollary of natural rights were staples of political theory; colonial publicists believed almost to a man in a higher law, a scheme of moral absolutes to be discovered and understood principally through the use of reason. The colonist who accepted the law of nature was more than likely to subscribe to these other teachings of this famous creed: the concept of man as an essentially good, sociable, educable creature; the historical or logical state of nature; the formation of society and government through an act of will, specifically through a contract; "Peace and Security," "the Publick Good," "the Happiness of the People," and "the preservation of the natural Rights of Mankind" as the chief ends of government; the retention by men who have entered society of the largest feasible portion of their natural rights (including the right to property) and natural equality; the instrument of majority rule as the one workable method of decision "among all Communities of civiliz'd Nations"; public office as a public trust, the doctrine that magistrates are servants rather than rulers of the people; and the great right of resistance (rarely if ever styled "rebellion" or "revolution") against rulers bent on tyranny or violation of the law of nature.

A favorite corollary of natural law was the concept of popular sovereignty. Colonial thinkers delighted to quote *Cato's Letters* on "the *sacred Priviledges of the People;* the *inviolable Majesty of the People;* the *awful Authority of the People,* and *the unappealable Judgment of the People.*" No less favored was the belief that government was "of all human Things the most inestimable Blessing that Mankind enjoy." The notion that government is at best a necessary evil found little if any response in colonial minds. Government, certainly free government, was good, beneficial, and popular, the product of purposeful men acting in pursuit of universal principles.

The second support of "Liberty, charming Liberty" was Whig constitutionalism. The principles and slogans of Whiggery were imported wholesale into colonial polemics and, until the very end of the colonial period, were more popular with the average colonist than were the principles of natural law and rights. The influence of English upon American political thought was in this instance overwhelming. The colonists sang continually these major themes of Whiggery: the English Constitution ("the best model of Government that can be framed by Mortals"); English rights ("GOD be thanked, we enjoy the Liberties of England"); balanced government ("the most compleat and regular, that has ever been contrived by the Wisdom of Man"); jury trial ("that firmest Barrier of English Liberty"); habeas corpus ("that inestimable jewel"); limited monarchy ("under the mild and gentle Administration of a *limited* Prince, every Thing looks cheerful and happy, smiling and serene"); and the malignity of arbitrary power (a state in which the "Sovereign Power is directed by the Passions, Ignorance & Lust of them that Rule").

They were equally pleased to sound the minor notes on rotation in office, annual Parliaments, free elections, fear of standing armies, liberty of the press, the curse of "placemen," the blessing of learned and upright judges, and the "baleful influence of Party." Political controversy in America before 1765 was carried on exclusively in the Whig idiom, with its devotion to the Glorious Revolution, its hatred of the Jacobites, and its consistent denunciation of the "popish doctrine of passive obedience and nonresistance." Conservatives might lay extra emphasis on the principles of balanced government and property rights, but this did not make them any the less Whiggish in conviction. "Before the revolution," Jefferson wrote, "we were all good Whigs, cordial in their free principles, and in their jealousies of the executive Magistrate."

The colonist had no need or urge to fawn upon English sensibilities. He was entirely sincere and straight in his own mind when, in defiance of absolute monarchies, he cried:

How much must an inhabitant of these Dispotick Governments envy an *English* man the Liberty he enjoys? . . . In such a Country, sure every Man in his right Senses would dwell if he could.

This did not mean that he must go to England to find liberty and happiness, for the colonies were improved extensions of England. Nor was English blood the condition of English liberty. A Pennsylvanian reminded his fellow freeholders:

Whether you be *English*, *Irish*, *Germans*, or *Swedes*, whether you be churchmen presbyterians, quakers, or of any other denomination of religion, whatsoever, you are by your residence, and the laws of your country, freemen and not slaves. You are entitled to all the liberties of *Englishmen* and the freedom of this constitution.

According to sound Whig doctrine, the antiquity of the English Constitution and liberties was their chief claim to devotion. As the colonists became increasingly conscious of natural law and rights, they began to set conformity to nature alongside antiquity as an explanation of the peculiar excellence of the English scheme. The printer of the *Connecticut Gazette* declared to his readers, "It is the glory of the British Government, that these natural Rights of Mankind, are secured by the Laws of the Land." The

English Constitution was the most accurate possible earthly model of the laws of nature; English rights were equally accurate reproductions of natural rights. The colonists could count no greater blessing, not even their natural situation, than their inheritance of the English form of government. A writer in one of the most American of newspapers asserted:

It has been a Question much controverted in the World, what Form of Government is best: And in what System . . . Liberty is best consulted and preserved. . . . There is no Form of Civil Government, which I have ever heard or read of, appears to me so well calculated, to preserve this Blessing, or to secure to its Subjects, all the most valuable Advantages of Civil Society, as the *English.* For in none that I have ever met with, is the Power of the Governors, and the Rights of the Governed, more nicely adjusted; or the Power which is necessary in the very Nature of Government to be intrusted in the Hands of some, by wiser Checks prevented from growing exorbitant.

The author of this Whiggish piece went on to say:

But neither the wisest Constitution, nor the wisest Laws, will secure the Liberty and Happiness of a People, whose Manners are universally corrupt.—He therefore is the truest Friend to the Liberty of his Country, who tries most to promote its Virtue.—And who so far as his Power and Influence extends, will not suffer a Man to be chosen into any Office of Power and Trust, who is not a wise and virtuous Man. . . .

The sum of all is—If we would most truly enjoy this Gift of Heaven—Let us become a VIRTUOUS PEOPLE:—Then shall we both deserve and enjoy it: While on the other Hand— If we are universally vicious, and debauched in our Manners—Though the Form of our Constitution, carries the Face of the most exalted Freedom, we shall in Reality be the most ABJECT SLAVES.

Here he put his finger upon the third requisite of liberty, expressing a belief, shared by most colonial publicists, that "there is an inseparable connection between publick virtue and publick happiness," and that liberty, the essence of happiness, can exist only among a truly virtuous people. The refinements of this aspect of political thought were many. Some colonists emphasized the dependence of virtue, and therefore of liberty, on the principles of religion. Others called upon parents, educators, and public writers "to paint Virtue in its most beautiful Colours." Still others, many of whom borrowed the idea consciously from *Cato's Letters*, asserted that "publick Men are the Patterns of Private; and the Virtues and Vices of the Governors become quickly the Virtues and Vices of the Governed." A common theme was the arraignment of the most baneful public vices: luxury and corruption. Readers of the newspapers were constantly reminded that "the Roman Virtue and the Roman Liberty expired together." Even more common was the celebration of the great public virtues: patriotism, public service, industry and frugality, justice, and integrity. Colonists were always delighted to hear, especially from English writers, that they were more virtuous than their elder brothers in England.

A favorite practice was to delineate, especially just before election time, the character of the good ruler or representative. In the last decade of the colonial period the ideal of the man of public virtue was made real in the person of William Pitt. The cult of this noblest of Whigs, "the Genius of England and the Comet of his Age," was well advanced toward idolatry at least five years before the Stamp Act. The greatest of "the great men of England," the last and noblest of the Romans, was considered the embodiment of virtue, wisdom, patriotism, and liberty. The presence of such a man in high places proved that government was sound and just; his departure or dismissal proved that it had turned corrupt and vicious. The art of government was just as simple as that. Political liberty was nothing more than the presence in the body politic of a substantial proportion of virtuous, liberty-loving men; it was, that is to say, a problem in ethics rather than economics.

To close the circle on the three elements of liberty, we should note that virtue, like the English Constitution, was considered an earthly version of the law of nature. As one writer phrased it, virtue "in its most general sense, consists in an exact observance of the Laws of Nature," which command that we "contribute as much as we can . . . to the Preservation and Happiness of Mankind in General." Liberty, he continued, "is a natural Power of doing, or not doing whatever we have a Mind, so far as is consistent with the Rules of Virtue and the established Laws of the Society to which we belong." Here in one brief passage is the colonial "party line": liberty —the final goal and sweetest fruit of nature, of virtue, and of the English Constitution. "The End of Government therefore, and the chief business of all wise and just Governours, is, to inforce the Observance of the Laws of Virtue or Nature."

Colonial political thinkers were English to the core, but this should not be taken to mean that they had no ideas or imagination of their own. The process of borrowing was highly selective. Trenchard, Gordon, Locke, Care, and Somers were imported and quoted because they answered the needs of the colonists; dozens of other writers, no less quotable and certainly no less English, were ignored or flatly rejected because they did not. Only that part of the whole English tradition which spoke of liberty got a warm welcome from this colonial people so intent upon liberty. And this part, too, was not accepted without changes in emphasis. Colonial thinkers paid special attention to principles that royal governors tended to play down: representation, freedom of press, equality, and jury trial.

At the same time, they came up with a few twists of their own. Agrarianism, the belief that the good men who make up the good state live and work in the country rather than the city, became increasingly popular in the eighteenth century. Long before Jefferson Americans were warning that the result of "clustering into Towns, is Luxury; a great and mighty Evil, carrying all before it, and crumbling States and Empires, into slow, but inevitable Ruin." Long before John Taylor they were proclaiming that "Agriculture is the most solid Foundation on which to build the Wealth and political Virtue of a Commonwealth." A second interesting development was the trend toward what we may properly call political pragmatism, toward the peculiar American insistence that liberty is to be judged by its fruits rather than by its inherent rationality or conformity to nature, and that at least one of the fruits of liberty is economic prosperity. A third variant was the American Mission, the belief that the colonies held a peculiar responsibility for the success of free government all through the world. The American version of the concept of the chosen people had its roots in Puritan Massachusetts. Said John Winthrop: "For we must consider that we shall be as a city upon a hill. The eyes of all peoples are upon us, so that if we shall deal falsely with our God in this work we have undertaken, we shall be made a story and a byword throughout the world." "God sifted a Whole Nation," cried William Stoughton in his election sermon of 1668, "that he might send Choice Grain over into this Wilderness." By the eighteenth century this sense of mission had been secularized and amplified. Liberty rather than true religion was to be the burden of America's teaching to the world. The American Mission gave added dignity to colonial speculations about political truth.

Students of our intellectual history will never agree finally on the year, or even the decade, when the English-Americans in the continental colonies became more American than English in thought and culture. The rub, of course, is the definition of "American," which is often used to denote an idea or artistic creation produced, however imitatively, by someone living in America, and as often to denote an idea or creation that is original or at least indigenous, one that could not be exactly duplicated anywhere else. If we adopt, as we probably should, the latter definition, we must acknowledge that there was very little genuinely American in colonial thought and culture. The influence of England—a blessing to the extent that it lent the colonists a helping hand and kept them from excessive insularity, a disservice to the extent that it choked off native creative impulses—was paramount, never more so than at the moment when the colonists put on their first show of purposeful resistance to English imperial policy. Addison and Steele, Gordon and Trenchard, Locke, Newton, Pope—the roll call of these idols of the colonial mind is a measure of American intellectual dependence on England.

Yet the dependence was that of an imitative and fast-growing younger brother rather than of a servile and stunted child. It must be emphasized again tha colonial borrowing of English institutions and ideas was selective, and that the chief criterion of selection was the usefulness of institution or idea to a people headed consciously in the direction of liberty. In all aspects of colonial thought, in science and education no less than in philosophy and political theory, the trend was to liberty, democracy, originality, and self-reliance. The men of the American settlements were a special breed of colonist, and theirs was accordingly a special brand of colonial culture.

Conclusion

The Second American Revolution Succeeds the First

On March 22, 1765, George III gave his royal assent to the Stamp Act, a stick of imperial dynamite so harmless in appearance that it had passed both houses of Parliament as effortlessly as "a common Turnpike Bill." Eleven years later, July 2, 1776, the Continental Congress resolved after "the greatest and most solemn debate":

That these United Colonies are, and, of right, ought to be, Free and Independent States; that they are absolved from all allegiance to the *British* crown, and that all political connexion between them, and the state of *Great Britain*, is, and ought to be totally dissolved.

In the tumultuous years between these two fateful acts the American colonists, at least a sufficient number of them, stumbled and haggled their way to a heroic decision: to found a new and independent nation upon political and social principles that were a standing reproach to almost every other nation in the world. Not for another seven years could they be certain that their decision had been sound as well as bold; only then would the mother country admit reluctantly that the new nation was a fact of life rather than an act of treason. The colonists were to learn at Brooklyn and Valley Forge that it was one thing to resolve for independence and another to achieve it.

Yet the resolution for independence, the decision to fight as a "separate and equal" people rather than as a loose association of remonstrating colonials, was as much the climax of a revolution as the formal beginning of one, and it is this revolution—the "real American Revolution"—that I have sought to describe in this book. By way of conclusion, I would think it useful to point briefly to those developments in the decade after 1765 that speeded up and brought to bloody conclusion "this radical change in the principles, opinions, sentiments, and affections" of the hitherto loyal American subjects of George III.

The progress of the colonies in these years was nothing short of astounding. Thanks to the fecundity of American mothers and the appeal of the American land, population increased from 1,850,000 in 1765 to more than 2,500,000 in 1776. America's troubles seemed only to make America more alluring; immigrants arrived in especially large numbers between 1770 and 1773. The westward pressure of 650,000 new colonists was, of course, enormous, and many new towns and settlements were planted in frontier lands east of the proclamation line of 1763. The sharp increase in population of the continental colonies lent support to arguments, especially popular after 1774, that Americans would some day outnumber Englishmen, and that there was "something absurd in supposing a continent to be perpetually governed by an island." Signs of increased wealth and well-being inspired other Americans to sing the glories of "a commerce out of all proportion to our numbers."

Far more significant than this material progress was the quickened influence of the "forces-behind-the-forces" I singled out in Chapter I. The English heritage, the ocean, the frontier, and imperial tension never worked so positively for political liberty as in this decade of ferment. Until the last days before independence the colonists continued to argue as Englishmen demanding English rights. The more they acted like Americans, the more they talked like Englishmen. Heirs of a tradition that glorified resistance to tyranny, they moved into political combat as English Whigs rather than American democrats, reminding the world that "it is the peculiar Right of Englishmen to complain when injured." The other basic forces were no less favorable to the swift advance of the spirit of liberty. In a situation that called desperately for accurate information, firm decisions, and resolute administration, the very distance between London and Boston frustrated the development of a viable imperial policy. In a situation that called no less desperately for colonial understanding of the imperial difficulties facing Crown and Parliament, the push to the frontier weakened the bonds of loyalty to an already too-distant land. And the Stamp Act and Townshend Acts forced most articulate colonists to reduce the old conflict of English and American interests to the simplest possible terms. Since some Englishmen proposed to consign other Englishmen to perpetual inferiority, was it not simply a question of liberty or slavery?

The forces that had long been working for political freedom underwent a sharp increase in influence. The ancient struggle between royal governor and popular assembly took on new vigor and meaning. The depths of ill feeling were plumbed in the maneuvers and exchanges of Governors Bernard and Hutchinson and the Massachusetts legislature. The colonial press engaged in more political reporting and speculation in the single year between June, 1765, and June, 1766, than in all the sixty-odd years since the founding of the *Boston News-Letter*. In early 1765 there were twenty-three newspapers in the colonies, only two or three of which were politically conscious; in early 1775 there were thirty-eight, only two or three of which were not. The spirit of constitutionalism and the demand for written constitutions also quickened in the course of the far-ranging dispute over the undetermined boundaries of imperial power and colonial rights. The word "unconstitutional," an essential adjunct of constitutionalism, became one of America's favorite words. Most important, the Stamp Act was a healthy spur to political awareness among all ranks of men. Wrote John Adams in 1766:

The people, even to the lowest ranks, have become more attentive to their liberties, more inquisitive about them, and more determined to defend them, than they were ever before known or had occasion to be; innumerable have been the monuments of wit, humor, sense, learning, spirit, patriotism, and heroism, erected in the several provinces in the course of this year. Their counties, towns, and even private clubs and sodalities have voted and determined; their merchants have agreed to sacrifice even their bread to the cause of liberty; their legislatures have resolved; the united colonies have remonstrated; the presses have everywhere groaned; and the pulpits have thundered.

The thundering pulpit, an old and faithful servant of American freedom, set out to demonstrate anew the affinity of religious and political liberty. Bumptious Protestantism vied with temperate rationalism as spurs to disestablishment and liberty of conscience. Conditions for the final triumph of unqualified religious liberty grew more favorable in this unsettled decade. So, too, did conditions of economic independence. The over-all state of the American economy lent impressive support to radical claims that the colonies would get along just as well, if not better, outside the protecting confines of British mercantilism. In wealth, resources, production, ingenuity, and energy the Americans were fast approaching the end of the colonial line.

The broad social trends I described in Chapter V continued through the pre-Revolutionary decade. In every colony the middle class formed the nucleus of the patriot party, and in Boston it attained a position of commanding political influence. The aristocracy split into opposing camps, but the Lees of Virginia and Livingstons of New York are reminders that a decisive share of patriotic leadership fell to the American aristocrat. The political storms of the decade, which deposited power in new hands in almost every colony, did much to stimulate social mobility and class conflict. The career of the Sons of Liberty attests the growing fluidity of colonial society; the uprisings of the "Paxton Boys" in Pennsylvania and the Regulators in North Carolina attest the heightened tensions of class and section.

Finally, the colonial mind took rapid strides forward in this period, not alone in the field of political thought. Deism, rationalism, and the scientific spirit claimed increasing numbers of men in positions of leadership. The cult of virtue enjoyed a vogue even more intense than in the colonial period. The arts showed new signs of indigenous strength. The sharp increase in the number of newspapers was matched by an even sharper increase in the output of books and pamphlets. Three new colleges opened their doors to eager students, and King's and the Philadelphia Academy instituted the first American medical schools. Despite all the shouting about English rights and ways, the colonial mind was growing steadily less English and more American. By the standards of the old world, it was a mind not especially attractive, not least because it was setting out at last to find standards of its own.

The American colonies moved fast and far between 1765 and 1776. While the King fumed, the ministry blundered, assemblies protested, mobs rioted, and Samuel Adams plotted, the people of the colonies, however calm or convulsed the political situation, pushed steadily ahead in numbers, wealth, self-reliance, and devotion to liberty. The peaceful revolution that had been gathering momentum from the time of the first settlements moved irresistibly to conclusion, and the fighting revolution could now begin. It could begin, moreover, with high hopes for its success. Blessed by a way of life that knew much freedom and held the promise of much more, the Americans, like the Englishmen who unseated James II, could make their revolution "a parent to settlement, and not a nursery of future revolutions." This was one colonial people that went to war for liberty knowing in its bones what liberty was.

INDEX